WISDOM OF PLACE

A Guide to Recovering the Sacred Origins of Landscape

ORO Editions
Publishers of Architecture, Art, and Design
Gordon Goff: Publisher

www.oroeditions.com
info@oroeditions.com

Published by ORO Editions

Author: Chip Sullivan & Elizabeth Boults
Book Design: Goldsmith Studio
Project Manager: Jake Anderson

10 9 8 7 6 5 4 3 2 First Edition

ISBN: 978-1-957183-19-0

Color Separations and Printing: ORO Editions Inc.
Printed in China.

ORO Editions makes a continuous effort to minimize the overall carbon footprint of its publications. As part of this goal, ORO, in association with Global ReLeaf, arranges to plant trees to replace those used in the manufacturing of the paper produced for its books. Global ReLeaf is an international campaign run by American Forests, one of the world's oldest nonprofit conservation organizations. Global ReLeaf is American Forests' education and action program that helps individuals, organizations, agencies, and corporations improve the local and global environment by planting and caring for trees.

CONTENTS

THE MINOR ARCANA 104

Water

Air

Wood

Earth

INTRODUCTION

Welcoming the Genius

Have you ever been alone in the woods and felt an eerie presence? Have you ever been puzzled by a sudden gust of wind or a bright flash of light or startled by the sound of your own voice echoing across the landscape? Do you sense that something magical dwells in the periphery of your vision? How do you explain these phenomena? Throughout human history, nature was long thought to be animated by unseen forces. The landscape was alive with deities and mystical entities who personified natural features and events. We ask, where have these gods and goddesses gone?

For millennia, earth spirits were venerated and worshiped as peoples across the globe altered the landscape in accord with what they believed to be the sacred qualities of place. Over time, as respect for the earth's unseen forces faded from modern consciousness, our rampant destruction of the environment intensified. Early peoples believed that the boundary between the physical world and the spiritual realm was not fixed. People came to know the essence of the deserts, mountains, seacoasts, plains, and forests where they lived, and developed narratives based on their awareness of the environment and their knowledge of its definitive patterns and processes. Cultural values were embodied in myths and folklore, informed by everyday experiences of the natural world. In this age of profound climate disruption and ecological upheaval, the time is ripe to reconsider and honor the sanctity of the land, to reimagine the role of the earth spirits in bringing forth a new era of environmental consciousness and care.

Every day of our lives we are in the presence of genius—what our ancestors called the *genius loci*, or spirit of place. But do we recognize it? Can we still hear the mountain, see the wind, feel the forest—without an app? At this moment in time, as wildfires rage, sea levels rise, species extinctions intensify, and a pandemic has shaken the world, human survival depends on our understanding the inherent wisdom of place. We must reawaken our sense of the earth's abiding intelligence and relearn the sacred language of nature.

To shed light on the ecological imperatives of our time, this book aims to help you rediscover the sacredness of the everyday landscapes around you. Drawn from the union of art, nature, and metaphysics, it presents some of the myths and legends of antiquity as they might be recognized by our modern society of earth-shapers. Through word and image, we reference the ecological and environmental concepts found at the core of traditional environmental knowledge and provide a new context for environmental engagement that merges the spiritual and phenomenological with the scientific and empirical. *Wisdom of Place* can be used by anyone—from creatives to spiritual seekers, landscape architects to coders—to call forth the voice of the *genius loci*, the spirit of place, and reveal the creative forces and hidden currents of nature.

Format of this Book

Wisdom of Place examines various expressions of the power of place through the narrative structure of the tarot. Our interest in tarot stems from its history as a storytelling practice based on archetypes of human consciousness. Developed centuries ago as an entertaining card game and evolving into a mystical practice of divination, the tarot employs a rich symbolic vocabulary. We adapt this allegorical framework by associating the meaning of traditional tarot figures with ideas, concepts, and manifestations of *genius loci* to expand the context of environmental consciousness in an original and captivating way.

The tarot is also a story of a journey to enlightenment. Similarly, in the quest for a more sustainable future, people need to cultivate a broader understanding of the earth's ecological systems as well as its spiritual essence. We use the tarot format as a creative catalyst to explore the meaning and symbolism of nature-based beliefs from around the world and their expression as a landscape lexicon. Recognizing and honoring the *genius loci*—the spirit of the landscape in which you live—is the first step in preserving its ecological integrity.

A typical tarot deck contains seventy-eight cards divided into two groups: the Major Arcana consisting of twenty-two cards, and the Minor Arcana consisting of fifty-six cards. ("Arcanum" means secret or mystery.) Traditionally, the Major Arcana comprise general themes and influences in life, while the Minor Arcana depict more specific encounters and situations along the journey. Our Major Arcana represent broad concepts and fundamental principles of environmental consciousness and their common expressions in global folklore. Our Minor Arcana represent specific elements and features of "sacred" landscapes. Like a conventional tarot, our Minor Arcana are subdivided into four suits of fourteen cards each, representing the elemental properties of Earth, Air, Water, and Wood. We took turns illustrating each card in our own artistic style to create a visual dialogue—Chip's watercolor renderings alternate with Elizabeth's hand-cut paper collages. We hope our work will lead you to rediscover a multitude of long overlooked landscape spirits and be inspired to find and create new meaning in your own sacred landscape.

Our Inspiration

Historically, across the globe, comprehending the spirit of place was a critical first step for people before they altered the environment to suit their needs. In looking at the contemporary built landscape one might wonder, where is the *genius* today… at the genius bar?! How might people better appreciate the inherent presence of place, and channel it to find meaning in their lived environments? In our work as artists, teachers, and landscape architects we champion the cause for a more sustainable and just society through practices that enrich both personal and environmental awareness. We have taught courses and presented workshops on the subject as well as organized "spirit walks" for people to rediscover the magic in the landscapes around them. *Wisdom of Place* is a result of our desire to share our passion with a broad audience.

As creative partners we also share a deep sensitivity to all aspects of *genius loci* as well as an appreciation for the serendipitous. This project can be considered a synthesis of the many profound coincidences that we have witnessed and recorded in our journals and sketchbooks. In our travels and in our own backyard, the practical magic of place has revealed itself to us in remarkable ways. For instance, several years ago, on a trip to Italy to research Renaissance gardens and villas we booked accommodations at a remote agriturismo near the towns of Assisi, Gubbio, and Perugia. Located in the scenic Umbrian foothills, the Abbazia di Vallingegno was a former Benedictine abbey. We are both extremely superstitious and hyper-attuned to the vagaries of nature. In order not to frighten each other we refrained from mentioning that late every night we both had been awakened by bright flashes of light outside the window. When we drove out along the cypress-lined entryway for the last time, we spotted a small shrine set into a little hollow that had gone unnoticed at the bottom of the hill. We stopped to do some sketches. The shrine was adjacent to a spring and decorated with freshly cut flowers.

Turning onto the main road, we saw up ahead a Franciscan monk with his thumb out. We looked at each other, and even though we never pick up hitchhikers, thought, *how can we not give this monk a lift?* As he settled into the backseat, we understood enough Italian to grasp that he wanted to give us a blessing. Appreciating the rarity of the circumstance, we agreed. He asked to be dropped off at the next intersection and got out of the car. We suddenly realized that we should have offered him a gratuity, but when we turned around, he was gone. Returning home, we learned that the abbey was once the site of a Roman temple to the *genio*. The name "vallingegno" stems from the Latin *valllis genii*, "valley of the spirit." Given our experiences of its ghostly lights, we were embarrassed to have missed the significance of the name of the place. Furthermore, we discovered that Saint Francis frequently visited the abbey on his pilgrimages to La Verna. No doubt a strange coincidence given the location of our hitchhiking Franciscan monk. This was one of the many experiences that set into motion our search for the greater meaning of *genius loci* and its potential to inspire environmental consciousness.

Re-enchanting the Natural World

How people value the earth and the environment is critical to the creation of a new, more sustainable design ethos. Current trends of virtual and augmented reality have removed people from direct contact with nature, replacing instinct, intuition, and first-hand experience as sources of knowledge and eliminating our need to understand the metaphysical forces of nature. Yet we still wish on stars, throw coins in fountains, and knock on wood, uncertain that there is not a correlation between our behavior and the phenomena of nature.

Landscapes are legendary. When at one with nature our senses are sharp, and our imaginations run wild. Humans instinctively perceive the immaterial power of the natural world to evoke serenity and joy, as well as fear and trepidation. Without authentic and tangible experience to draw from in today's virtual world we are in danger of losing our ability to tell these stories, to make sense of the landscapes around us, to appreciate the wisdom of place.

We consider the seventy-eight images in this book as pathways to enchantment, artful representations of metaphors that help realign spiritualism with environmentalism. We explain each figure's significance as a component of nature and of human imagination. You can interact with the content to gain new knowledge about natural systems, to find personal inspiration, to stimulate creative thinking, and to encourage positive action. We hope that *Wisdom of Place* not only enriches your environmental literacy but also restores your sense of wonder at the world.

ACKNOWLEDGMENTS

Throughout the lengthy gestation of this project the encouragement and wisdom of very many people sustained us. Our gratitude extends to all who journeyed with us.

Wisdom of Place was initially inspired by a design assignment in Chip's seminar on Sacred Landscapes at UC Berkeley in 2018. Students were required to illustrate four different environmental themes on a single page with one-word captions. When pinned up together on the studio wall, the format appeared to Chip like tarot cards. The students enthusiastically embraced Chip's idea of creating and producing tarot cards to communicate their own interpretations of sacred landscapes. We are grateful to all our students for the spark that they continually provide us, and for the positive energy that ignited our passion to develop this project with a wider scope. In particular, we thank Megan Bradley, Stan Kim, and Kateryna Dronova for organizing and overseeing the publication of the students' decks. They are amazing. Additional support from the Beatrix Farrand Endowment through the Department of Landscape Architecture and Environmental Planning at University of California, Berkeley, was also instrumental in bringing this project to fruition. As our deadline loomed, the research assistance provided by Olivia Haag and Clarissa Xiao was vital to our timely completion of the manuscript.

We were excited to have the opportunity to present this project in its early stages to a national audience at the American Society of Landscape Architects 2019 Conference on Landscape. We appreciate all who participated in our interactive workshop, and especially thank Susan Apollonio, ASLA's former Education Programs Director, for suggesting we propose the session. We are also grateful to Dr. Zuzana Ambrožová for inviting us to conduct a similar workshop at Mendel University in Czechia. Both experiences were extremely valuable in shaping this project.

Our interest in the power of *genius loci* is shared by a large community of friends and colleagues. We are indebted to Marisa Naughton and Siobhan Hussey for their honest commitment to the spirit of place and for introducing us to Jessica Kung Dreyfus and the Make Conscious collective. Their work to make conscious creation the basis of professional practice truly motivates us. We are also grateful to Jessica for referring us to literary coach and wellness instructor Lisa Weinert and her Narrative Healing™ group.

Lisa helped us find our voice as writers and provided invaluable advice on how to bring our work into the world of publishing in the 21st century. Within this circle we owe thanks to Barry Sutton for his initial design of our website thewidsomofplace.com, and to Jennifer Kurdyla for her thoughtful edits on our initial book proposal. For providing feedback on early versions of our proposal, we would especially like to thank Tamara Birdsall, Allison Bryant, Cindy Boults, Elaine Boults, Hélène Côté, Pamela Cunningham, Cyndy Duade, Marybeth Harasz, Diane Ivanovic, and Haven Kiers. We are grateful for your belief in this project. We are indebted to Jiaqi "Lucky" Li and Kevin "Renjun" So for their expert elaboration of our website design and social media graphics. Our heartfelt gratitude extends to the fabulous Jenny Frenkel, of Intuitive Relations PR, for her exceptional guidance with marketing and promotion initiatives.

Thank you to publisher Gordon Goff and managing editor Jake Anderson at ORO Editions for making our vision a reality. We are thrilled to be part of their catalog of outstanding titles. Additional thanks to Bernadette Esposito for her patience and expertise as copy editor. This beautiful book that you are holding in your hands was designed by the phenomenal team of Amanda Goldsmith and Dominic Vadra-Edwards at Goldsmith Studio. Their astounding creativity and imagination brought life to these pages in ways which we could only dream. A special shout out to Lucy Yuan for creating the additional maps, diagrams, and illustrations that supplement the major arcana. Amanda and Dom also contributed digital artwork to that section. We admire and appreciate the many talents of our creative crew.

Many others beyond those mentioned in this brief chronology contributed to the evolution of *Wisdom of Place*; we value and appreciate their input. Last, but certainly not least, we acknowledge and honor the genius of the land on which we are fortunate to live.

MAJOR ARCANA

To practitioners, the Tarot is alive. The cards present situations from which readers can develop their intuitive sense in response to ever changing circumstances of life. In a sense, the Tarot is what you want it to be. The twenty-two cards of the traditional Major Arcana suggest encounters that in succession can help promote one's consciousness of self and world. The Major Arcana illustrated in *Wisdom of Place* were inspired by a similar objective of helping readers make connections between themselves and their environments. Our cards locate familiar knowledge within the esoteric, and vice-versa.

CORRESPONDENCES

0	The Green Man	**0**	The Fool
I	The Biosphere	**I**	The Magician
II	The Doors of Perception	**II**	The High Priestess
III	Pachamama	**III**	The Empress
IV	Organic Proportion	**IV**	The Emperor
V	The Geometer	**V**	The Hierophant
VI	The Green Woman	**VI**	The Lovers
VII	Alignments	**VII**	The Chariot
VIII	The Hydrologic Cycle	**VIII**	Justice
IX	Deep Ecology	**IX**	The Hermit
X	Green Mandala	**X**	The Wheel of Fortune
XI	Geomancy	**XI**	Strength
XII	Axis Mundi	**XII**	The Hanged Man
XIII	Metamorphosis	**XIII**	Death
XIV	The Tree of Life	**XIV**	Temperance
XV	Koyaanisqatsi	**XV**	The Devil
XVI	Ecotones	**XVI**	The Tower
XVII	Polaris	**XVII**	The Star
XVIII	The Moon	**XVIII**	The Moon
XIX	The Sun	**XIX**	The Sun
XX	Closed Loop	**XX**	Judgement
XXI	Genius Loci	**XXI**	The World

0

THE GREEN MAN

Spring drew on...and a greenness grew over those brown beds, which, freshening daily, suggested the thought that Hope traversed them at night, and left each morning brighter traces of her steps.

Charlotte Brontë, *Jane Eyre*, 1847

Our story of the search for wisdom of place begins with the Green Man. His character is based on the protagonist known as The Fool, who is traditionally represented by the primary card of the major arcana in the tarot allegory. Like the Fool, the Green Man is about to undertake a journey with confidence and faith. He is poised to step off the precipice and into the magical realm of the *genius loci*. The precipice represents the edge of the known world, the border of the regions in which dwell the hidden forces of nature.

The Green Man is a folkloric forest figure typically portrayed with attributes of both wild nature and human nature. Garbed in leaves and branches, the historical character remains vivid in our collective imaginations, sharing traits with Dionysus and Pan as well as with Robin Hood and "Jack-in-the-Green"—who appears to this

Dionysus was the Greek god of agricultural productivity and renewal based on the myth of his rebirth. Like his Roman counterpart Bacchus, he became known as the god of wine and was often associated with sensational festivals of abandon that took place in nature.

day at May Day celebrations throughout Britain. In myths and legends from around the world, the Green Man is often depicted as a nature spirit, a god of fertility and a symbol of rebirth who personifies the mysteries of the spring season. Metaphorically, the Green Man represents the imperative of environmental awareness, the subconscious desire for an agitator of the "green" revolution today.

Costumed in leaves and branches, the Jack-in-the-Green character emerged in the 18th century when milkmaids and later chimney sweeps created elaborate floral decorations to celebrate the onset of spring.

0

THE GREEN MAN

I

THE BIOSPHERE

Humankind has not woven the web of life. We are but one thread within it. Whatever we do to the web, we do to ourselves. All things are bound together. All things connect.

Attributed to Duwamish and Suquamish leader Si'ahl (Chief Seattle), 1854

Like the Magician of tarot lore who is a conduit between the known and unknown and the inner and outer worlds, the Biosphere represents a consciousness of the harmony of the universe—"as above, so below." The Biosphere is the zone around the surface of the earth that contains all living matter. It extends from the inner reaches of the atmosphere, about six miles above the earth, to the lower depths of the oceans, about six miles below the earth's surface; its relative width is often compared to the skin of an apple. Within this self-supporting layer live the smallest microscopic bacteria as well as the largest animal species.

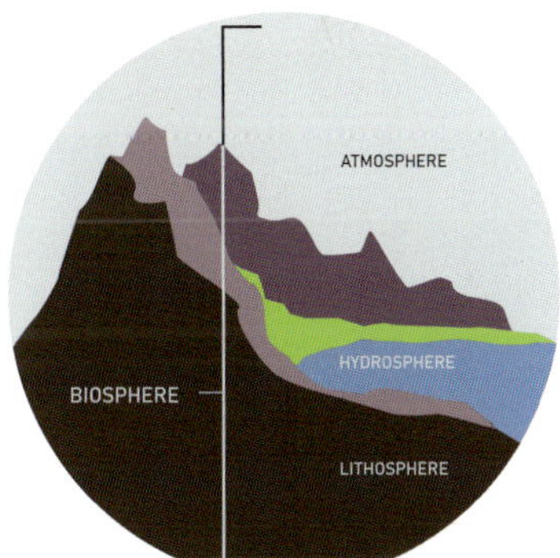

The layers of the relatively thin biosphere include the Lithosphere (the Earth's rocky crust and outer mantle), the Hydrosphere (oceans and waterways), and a portion of the atmosphere called the Troposphere. All matter in this system is continually recycled through the transfer of energy inputs from the sun.

Stories and legends from Indigenous peoples around the world tell of the literal and figurative links between the earth and the heavens, between the microcosm and the macrocosm, embodied by the Biosphere.

For example, in Native Hawaiian cosmology, the union of Papahānaumoku, the earth mother and goddess of the underworld, with Wākea, the sky father, created the sacred islands and atolls from which all life originates. Recognizing the mutual dependence of all the Earth's ecosystems as well as the interconnections between the material and spiritual realms is fundamental to the realization of environmental sustainability.

The complexity of the Biosphere is illustrated here through a dynamic collage composed from terrestrial maps, solar charts, engineering calculations, and illustrations of vegetation and architecture. The hand holding a wand is a reminder that our actions and interventions have consequences, intended and unintended. The energy and visual flow of the illustration evokes the bond between the earth and the heavens, and implies, ultimately, a connection between thought and deed.

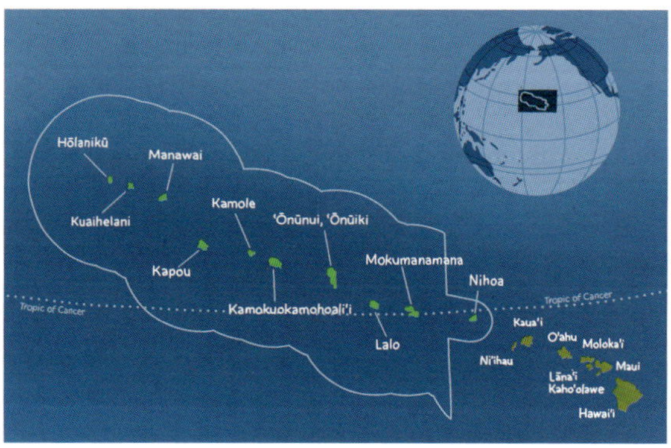

Covering over 500,000 square miles and home to more than 7,000 species, the Papahānaumokuākea Marine National Monument is the largest conservation area in the US. It is the only UNESCO World Heritage Site in the US that is recognized for both its natural and cultural significance.

I

THE BIOSPHERE

II

THE DOORS OF PERCEPTION

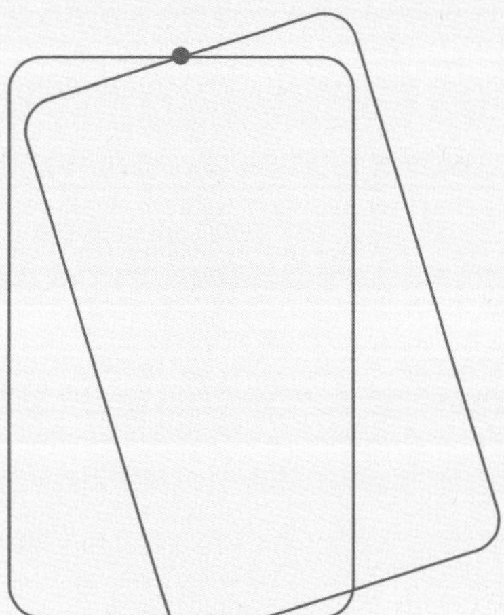

If the doors of perception were cleansed everything would appear to man as it is, infinite.

William Blake, *The Marriage of Heaven and Hell*, 1790

The High Priestess of the traditional tarot is represented here as the Goddess Isis watching over the doors of perception. Mystical knowledge, framed by palm trees symbolic of Egyptian pillars, is ultimately attained by passing through this threshold. Planted on both sides, pomegranates represent the fruitfulness of a spiritual life. Over the doorway a curtain billows in the wind, at times revealing and at other times obscuring the ultimate destination: a temple shrouded by a grove of palm trees. As dappled light reflects off its walls, the temple is sited on a crescent-shaped island. The isle is separated from the mainland by a flowing river. These aesthetic elements of the portal, palm grove, pomegranate orchard, and crescent-shaped island symbolize wisdom, time, and rebirth.

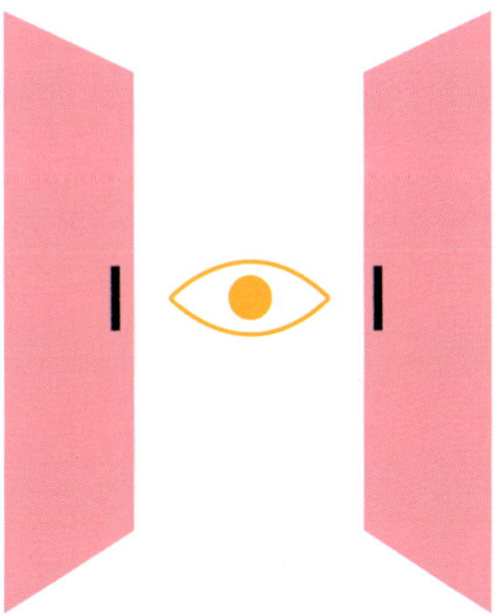

In Ayurvedic tradition, as in many other belief systems, the third eye (located in the center of your forehead) is the chakra of perception, intuition, and heightened awareness. Vision extends beyond the physical world outside the doors of perception.

Authors William Blake (1757-1827) and Aldous Huxley (1894-1963) both used the doorway as a metaphor for attaining higher consciousness. Similarly, Carlos Castaneda, in his book *Tales of Power*, presented the concept of the threshold as the border between the everyday reality of the known world and the unfathomable mystery of perception and intuition. These "in-between" spaces of passage and exchange are often referred to as liminal spaces, where profound transition and transformation can occur. Beliefs in guardian spirits and deities associated with boundaries and thresholds can be found in cultures across the globe.

Symbolic of the perfection of heaven, the circular Moon Gate in traditional Chinese gardens frames a view and marks the transition from one space to another. As you pass through the gate you move through layers of time, meaning, and mystery.

II
THE DOORS OF PERCEPTION

III

PACHAMAMA

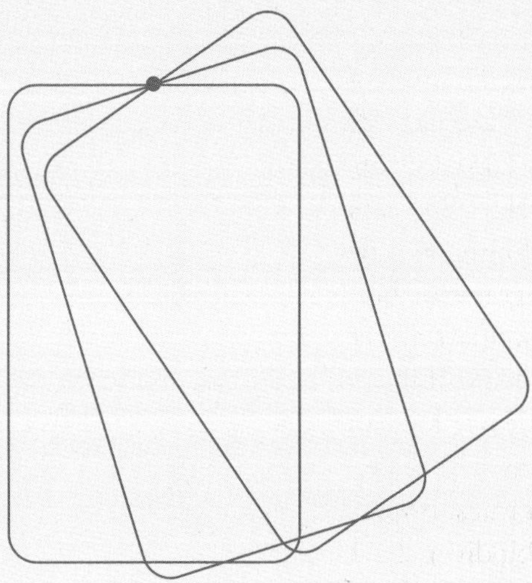

But the Earth is wise. It has given itself into the keeping of all, and all are therefore accountable.

Alice Walker, "Everything is a Human Being," in *Living by the Word*, 1989

The Empress occupies the third position in the sequence of a traditional tarot deck. We have associated her characteristics with Pachamama, goddess of the earth in Andean culture and Inca mythology. Illuminated by the heavens she reigns over all geographies of the world, assuring abundance and fertility to all the earth's biomes. A biome is a geographic area that supports a specific community of flora and fauna dependent on particular climatic conditions. As climates are changing around the world, biomes are shifting and deteriorating. General categories of biomes comprise forests, grasslands, deserts, tundra, and aquatic regions; within a biome exist a variety of ecosystems and habitats. With their warm temperatures and high precipitation rates, tropical forests have the greatest biodiversity. The Amazon rainforest supports more than three

Biomes are regions around the world with similar climatic conditions that support specific plant and animal life. The biomes illustrated here can be subdivided even further based on more detailed environmental factors.

million species, yet faces the greatest risk of loss from deforestation, particularly on Indigenous lands.

Shown in this illustration are references to Pachamama as a conception of the feminine divine—a radiant being enveloping the earth with compassion and natural beauty. Amidst a cosmic gradient, she embraces the totality of life in every biome. In the mountainous countries and agricultural economies of South America, Pachamama is often celebrated with a traditional festival of thanksgiving for the bounty that the earth provides. A shaman prepares an offering of food to give back to the mother in appreciation of how she nourishes her people. Pachamama represents a balance and reciprocity between the spiritual and the material, an alliance rather than a division of nature and culture.

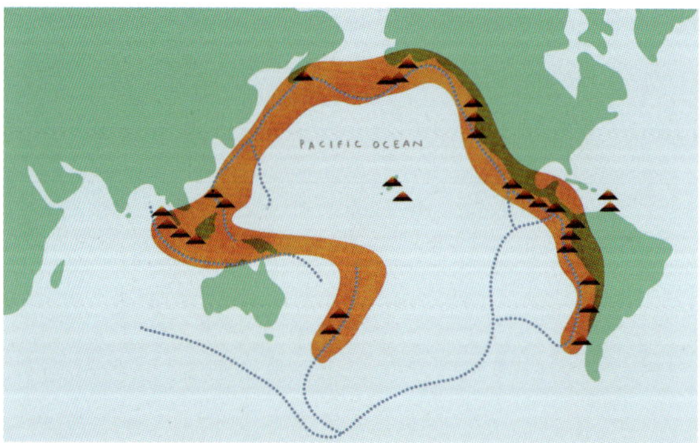

The Andes are part of the chain of mountains around the Pacific Ocean known as the "Ring of Fire," which is the world's largest zone of active volcanoes and earthquakes. In Andean folkore, Pachamama is believed to produce earthquakes if she is displeased with humans' care of the environment.

III
PACHAMAMA

IV

ORGANIC PROPORTION

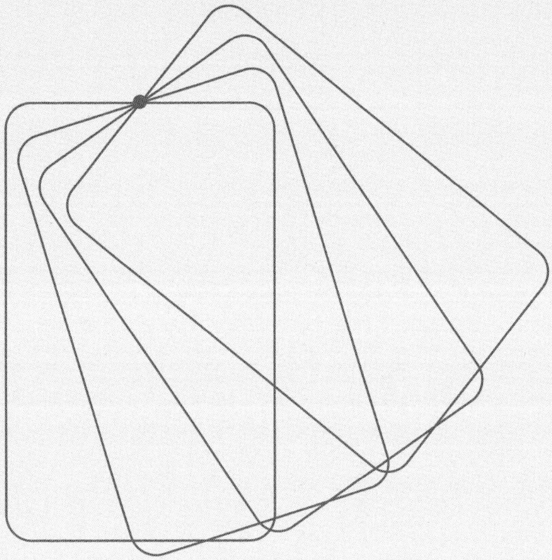

If we look closely at a flower and likewise at other natural and manmade creations, we find a unity and an order common to all of them.

Gyorgy Doczi, *The Power of Limits*, 1981

In the traditional tarot, the Emperor represents aspects of rule and control. We've extrapolated this meaning to explore a new canon of proportion based on organic growth. One of the most important and earliest systems of measurement ever devised was the ancient Egyptian "cubit." The basis for the cubit was the proportions of the human body. The standard cubit was equivalent to the length of a person's forearm from the elbow to the tip of the middle finger. One standard cubit equaled the length of six palms of the human hand, and one "digit" was the length of one human finger. Some of the world's most magnificent, enigmatic, and spectacular structures arose from this humble proportioning system.

Queen Hatshepsut's temple in the Nile Valley demonstrates bilateral symmetry. The central axis is formed by a long causeway that extends from the river to the western foothills. Ramps lead through a series of colonnaded terraces that appear to be carved out of the mountain.

In Egyptian legend, the ibis-headed god Thoth is credited with the invention of geometry—the foundation of proportion and scale. We illustrate the tools of Egyptian measurement in the hieroglyphics shown below the image of Thoth. At the base of the illustration is a cubit rod inscribed with incremental units. The digit, emerging from a human hand, points the way to a "green" future.

Our vision of an alternative system of proportion is based on natural patterns of efflorescence—how a plant develops from seed germ to final form. The seed germ depiction is inspired by the organic designs of American architect Louis Sullivan (1856-1924). Sullivan believed that design should be alive and arise from the organic patterns of nature and thus animate the spirit of the building.

The intricately woven foliage and tracery in Louis Sullivan's architectural ornament create an organic geometry that continuously mediates between the built and the natural.

IV

ORGANIC PROPORTION

V

THE GEOMETER

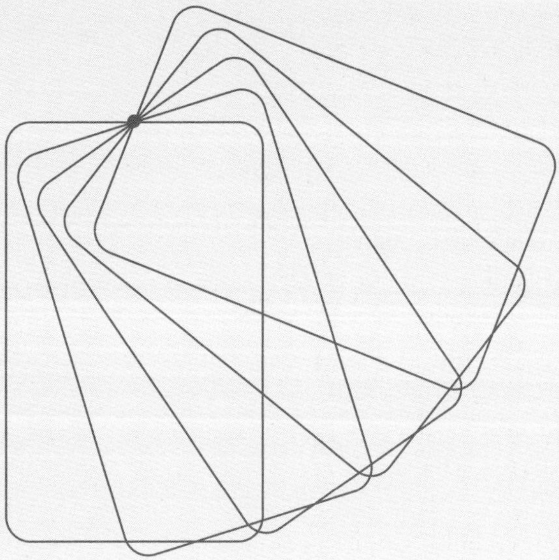

Geometry is the archetype of the beauty of the world.

Johannes Kepler (1571-1633), German astronomer

The Hierophant occupies the fifth position in the sequence of a traditional tarot deck. We represent the Hierophant's attributes of order and wisdom in the figure of the Geometer. The roots of the word "geometry" come from the Greek terms for "earth" and "measure." For thousands of years humans have "taken measures" to try to understand their place in the world and the place of their world in the cosmos. Our illustration of the Geometer references a few of the ways that people have employed geometry to understand spirit-of-place: the overlapping vectors of a Tibetan cosmic mandala, the orbits of the twelve constellations of the zodiac, the study of polyhedrons by Italian Renaissance artists, and the symmetrical growth patterns of plants and flowers.

The seeds in a Sunflower head express the Golden Spiral, a series of numbers known as the Fibonacci Sequence, where each number is the sum of the two numbers before it, for example, 1, 2, 3, 5, 8, 13, 21…

Geometry links reason with imagination and beauty. Throughout human history numbers have held a mystical power to peoples across the world. In many cultures, mathematics was believed to be a secret language capable of revealing divine knowledge. "Sacred geometry" refers to the idea that a certain proportional relationship is universal and can be found in all things. Known as the "golden section," and the "divine proportion" the number 1.618 (named "phi" after the ancient Greek sculptor Phidias) is expressed by a ratio that is found in nature as well as in art, architecture, music, and other forms. The spiral of seeds in a sunflower head and the spiral of chambers in a nautilus shell are common examples; the formation of weather systems, viruses, and crystals also illustrate the pattern.

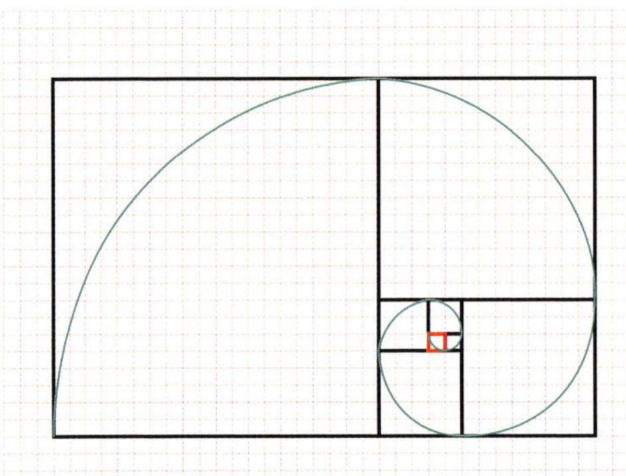

Phi is expressed in the proportions of the Golden Rectangle, where the long side divided by the short side is the same ratio as the short side (now the side of a square) divided by the "leftover" segment of the long side. This ratio can repeat to form beautiful patterns.

V

THE GEOMETER

VI

THE GREEN WOMAN

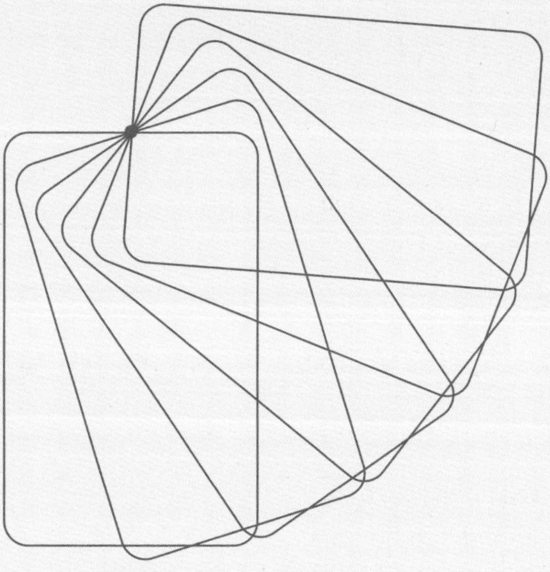

Shall I not have intelligence with the earth? Am I not partly leaves and vegetable mould myself?

Henry David Thoreau, *Walden*, 1854

The union of the Green Woman with the Green Man represents the traditional tarot symbol for the Lovers. The conventional interpretation shows the couple secure in a paradise garden, expressing the harmony and balance of a cosmic alliance. While the history and mythology of the Green Man has been well recognized in global cultural studies, the Green Woman's past is much less known; she has languished in semi-obscurity, suppressed, and looming in the dark recesses of human consciousness. We interpret her reemergence into the world as symbolic of ecological renewal and restoration. Forming bonds with each other and with the wider animal and plant kingdom can be a powerful force of positive ecological change.

The goddess Tara is believed to have sprung from a lotus flower growing in a lake formed by a tear from the bodhisattva. She is shown sitting on an open lotus and holding a closed lotus, symbolizing the balance of day and night.

The Green Tara is a female deity in several Buddhist traditions, a manifestation of compassion and wisdom, who actively supports healthy relationships. As green is the color associated with wood, she is also recognized as a forest dweller. Sitting atop a lotus flower, she radiates healing green light from the seed found at her heart.

Our illustration depicts two vegetal entities rising out of the fertile earth from acorns sprouting beneath an oak tree. Their combined energy creates a hypothetical new species of oak which is imbued with the superpowers of photosynthetic production, transpiration, atmospheric cleansing, and wildlife habitat generation.

There are more than 500 species of the oak genus, Quercus, worldwide. It is one of the oldest and longest living trees on earth, capable of supporting a wide and diverse range of life from large animals to microscopic fungi.

VI
THE GREEN WOMAN

VII

ALIGNMENTS

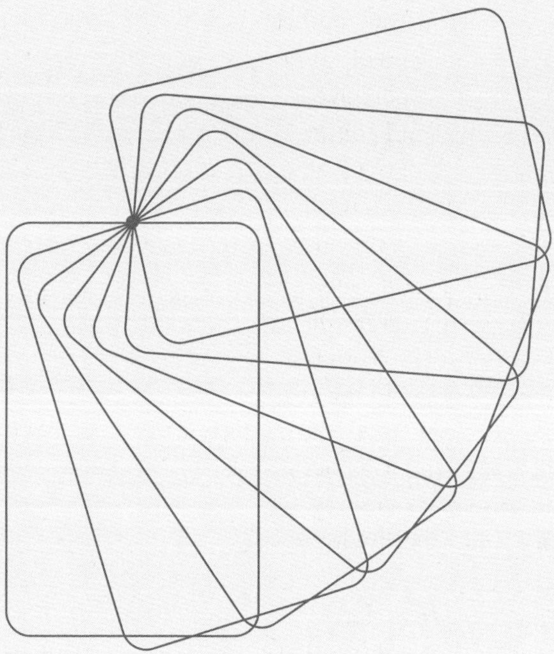

Over every mountain there is a path, although it may not be seen from the valley.

Theodore Roethke (1908-1963), American poet

The Chariot is the seventh card in the sequence of a traditional tarot deck and, as the name implies, symbolizes travel. We emphasize the path itself as the integral aspect of any journey, and call attention to the paths or lines of connection that people have perceived between certain natural and cultural forms in the landscape throughout history. Across time and space, humans have been guided by their awareness of various geological, hydrological, and astronomical features, and navigated a course of travel according to what they believed were paths of sacred energy embedded in the earth's ancient memory. "Alignments" are manifestations of these patterns of association and relationship that help us position ourselves, physically and spiritually, in the world.

Songlines are maps that for millennia have been created by Indigenous peoples of Australia to visually communicate traditional knowledge of place. The abstract symbols and geometric patterns trace the journey of the ancestral spirits who created the land, the sea, and all life.

Ley lines, songlines, fairy paths, spirit tracks, and geoglyphs are some examples of alignments. These patterns result from centuries, if not millennia, of human activity and use of the land based on a community's accumulated knowledge of their environment. Alignments represent a connection to place, an awareness of the *genius loci* that extends beyond one's immediate surroundings. Energy paths are not always straight lines; they can represent the pattern and flow of a specific geography. Experienced dowsers are able to detect an alignment. We interpret alignments as paths of spiritual energy with a landscape lineage.

The composition of this image makes visual reference to different ways in which people discern relationships between time, space, and energy.

Geoglyphs are images and symbols incised in the earth typically of a monumental scale. The Nazca Lines of Peru date from the 6th century BCE and depict figures such as spiders, hummingbirds, and monkeys that extend for hundreds of feet across the dry river bed.

VII

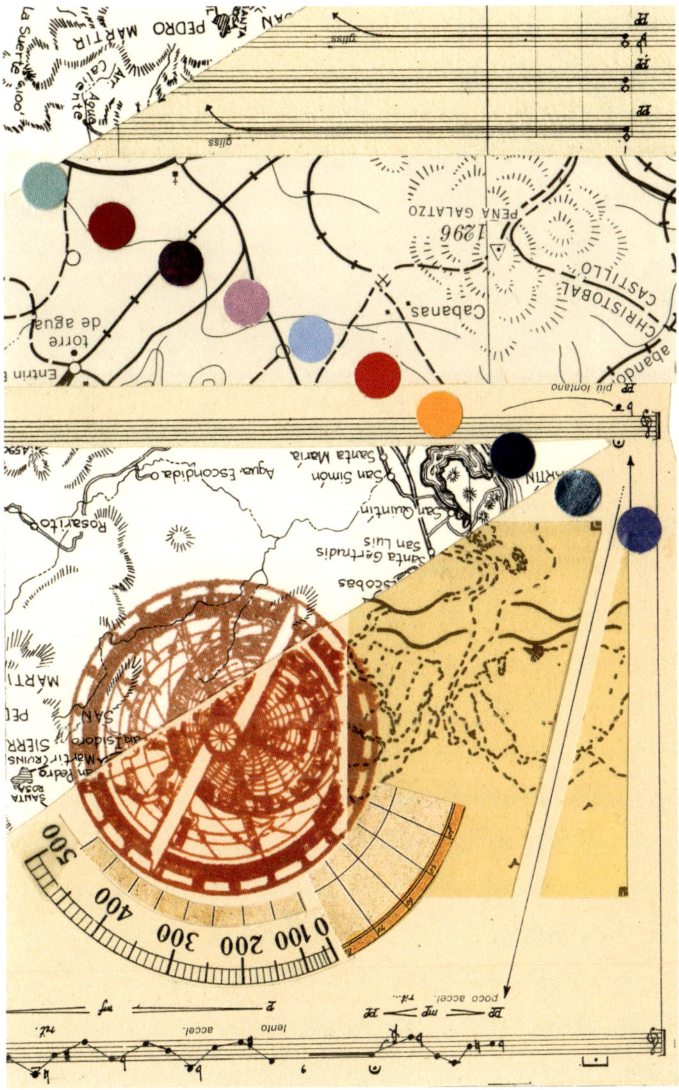

ALIGNMENTS

VIII

THE HYDROLOGIC CYCLE

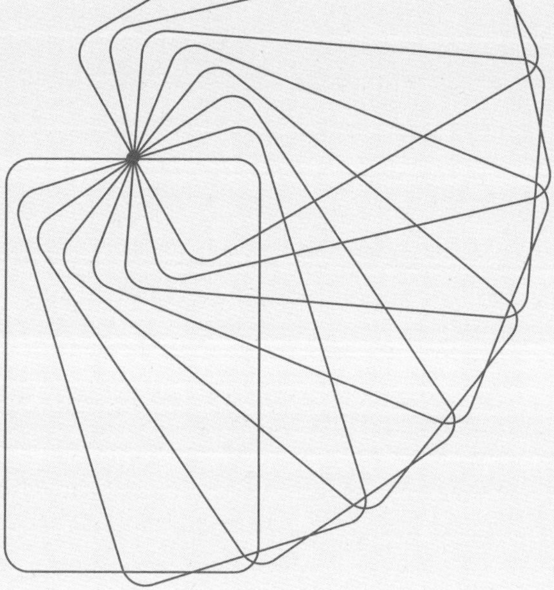

Water is the driving force of all nature.

Leonardo Da Vinci (1452–1519)

Justice, the eighth card in tarot tradition, is often shown holding her iconic balance scale. We associate this concept of dynamic equilibrium with the function and performance of the Hydrologic Cycle. Through processes of precipitation, evaporation, and transpiration, water moves from the earth's atmosphere to its surface and back again. We use the alchemical terms "Horsum" and "Seorsum" to explain the Hydrologic Cycle. Horsum, understood as "approaching movement," is illustrated by condensation (clouds) and precipitation (rain). In opposition is Seorsum, or "receding movement." Evaporation is the primary pathway in which water changes from its liquid state back into atmospheric vapor.

Water figures prominently in many cultures' mythologies and cosmologies.

As an artist and hydraulic engineer, Leonardo DaVinci studied the force and flow of water throughout his career.

Due to its fluid and inconstant properties, and its ability to change states, water is often associated with perpetual cycles of transformation and renewal. Figuratively, and literally, periods of drought may follow periods of flood, and vice versa. An empty well will be recharged and a full well drained. A balanced ecosystem requires knowledge of how these metaphorical principles are manifested in the landscape.

At the summit of the illustration is the Moon, one of the major forces powering Earth's water bodies. In the center of the image is the Sun, creating a central axis. Rain falls from clouds and turns the parched, dry landscape into a fruitful green oasis; water descends in regional watersheds defined by natural geological and topographical boundaries, flowing from creeks to streams to rivers, eventually feeding into large bodies of water.

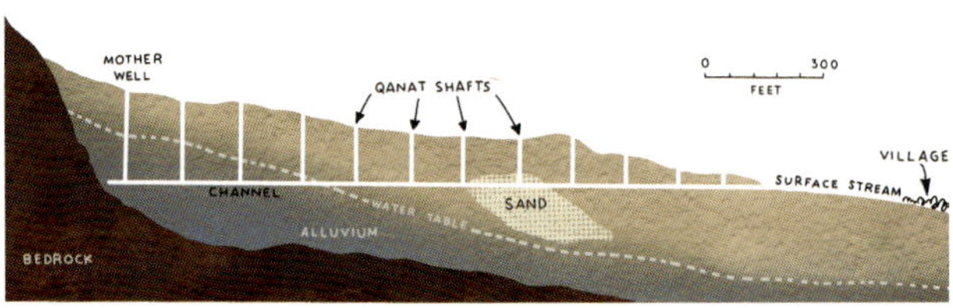

A *qanat* is an underground aqueduct developed by the ancient Persians to bring water from the mountains to the desert. The circular air vents formed during construction trace a path to the oasis.

VIII
SURSUM
HORSUM
DEORSUM
SEORSUM
THE HYDROLOGIC CYCLE

IX

DEEP ECOLOGY

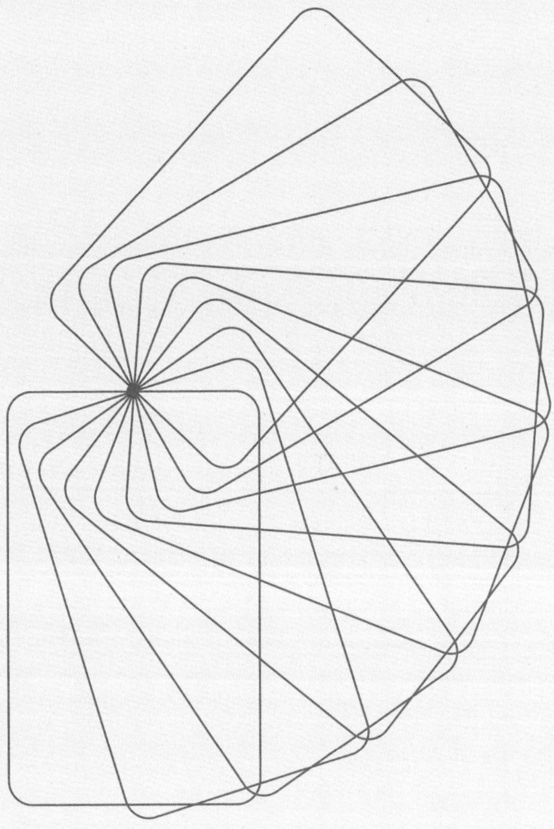

We are spiritual beings having a human experience.

Jane Goodall, *Reason for Hope: A Spiritual Journey*, 1999

The Hermit traditionally is the ninth card of the major arcana. As indicative of the search for consciousness that lies at the roots of one's reality, we have expressed the Hermit as embodying the concept of Deep Ecology. Deep Ecology is a philosophical position that argues for the value of a holistic consideration of the web of life, one in which humans are not at the center. "Biocentrism" is a similar term that refers to the belief in the equal value and purpose of all living beings; deep ecology extends the frame to include the worth of entire habitats and ecosystems, encompassing all nature. Supporters of Deep Ecology paint humans as just one part of the picture.

Many governments have granted rights to environmental systems. In 2008, Ecuador amended their constitution to recognize the rights of all nature.

An ecosystem is an interconnected web wherein all living and non-living matter are dependent on each other. One path of energy transfer throughout the web is the food chain.

In 2017, "environmental personhood" was granted to the Ganges and Yamuna rivers in India and the Whanganui River in New Zealand. In 2019, Bangladesh (home to the world's largest delta ecosystem) gave all its rivers the same legal protection as humans. Undoubtedly difficult to enforce, these legislations are a positive step toward greater environmental awareness and shared responsibility of the earth's health and well-being.

Our illustration captures the intricacy and richness of the plant and animal kingdom that exists beyond an anthropocentric perspective.

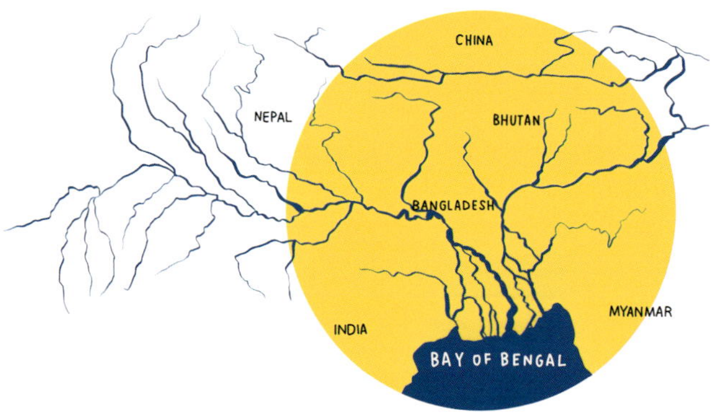

The Ganges-Brahmaputra delta is the largest delta system in the world, fanning out along the Bay of Bengal coast for over 200 miles.

IX

DEEP ECOLOGY

X

GREEN MANDALA

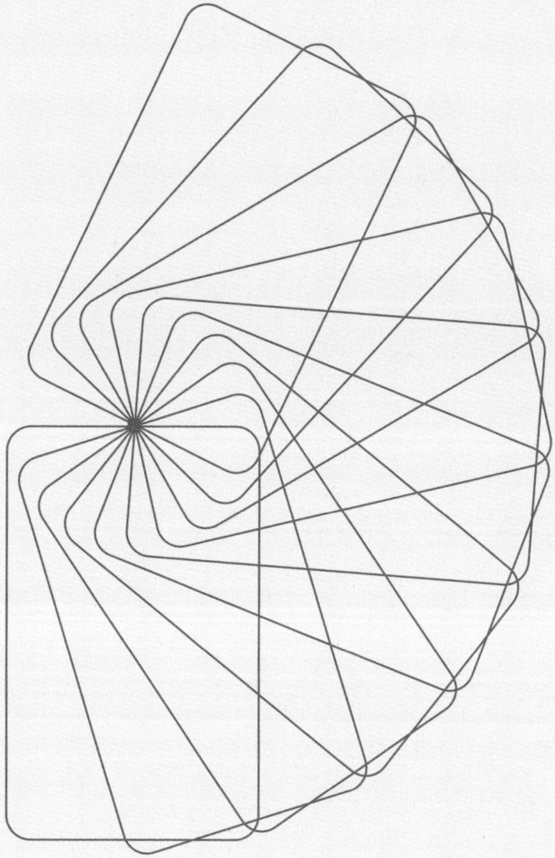

So what is discord at one level of your being is harmony at another level.

Alan Watts (1915-1973), English writer and philosopher

In a traditional tarot deck the Wheel of Fortune represents the universe and its interconnections. The symbol promotes the idea of centering and of cooperation with the fates. We represent these qualities in the form of a Green Mandala using the geometry of the Hindu Sri Yantra. Composed by nine triangles (four pointed up and five pointed down) enclosed within a circle, the Sri Yantra represents a union of body and universe. The opposing positions of the triangles symbolize the contrasting forces that simultaneously balance the universe: diversity and unity. The triads represent the harmonic cycles of creation, manifestation, and dissolution.

Mandala is the Sanskrit term for circle. The Green Mandala shown here is set within a halo of sunflower petals. The upward and downward interlocking triangles formed by

The form of a flower imitates the form of a mandala. Studying the circular pattern of petals and the development from bud to blossom can aid meditation.

deciduous and coniferous plants, respectively, are indicative of biomass. The Green Mandala floats below an electrically charged atmosphere of lightning and above the living soil. The green triangles are a manifestation of the dynamic forces of nature, and a symbol of change.

The Green Mandala recognizes the interplay of patterns at the macro and micro scales. By meditating on this diagram, one is drawn to the pulsating force of nature's botanical energy. Positive energy radiates out from the center and back into one's own consciousness, which can be redirected out into the landscape for the health and well-being of the environment.

A fractal is a pattern that repeats itself indefinitely or "scales up" in a way that the entire structure is geometrically similar to its smallest unit. In nature, fractals can be found in snowflakes, coastlines, and dendritic patterns of rivers.

X

GREEN MANDALA

XI

GEOMANCY

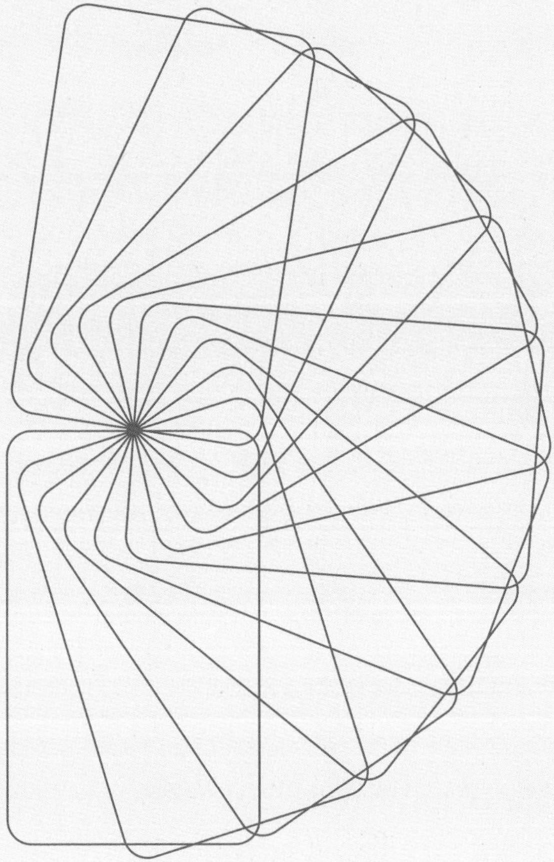

If you want to find the secrets of the universe, think in terms of energy, frequency and vibration.

Nikola Tesla, Serbian-American engineer (1856-1943)

We represent Strength, the eleventh card of the major arcana, as an expression of the principles of Geomancy. Geomancy is an ancient practice of divination, or prediction, based on interpretation of terrestrial forces. We illustrate these as currents of potential and fields of energy embodied in the earth that can be detected in various ways. Feng shui (the Chinese art of auspicious placement), Vastu shastra (the Ayurvedic system of harmonious alignment), and dowsing (the tradition of using an instrument to find underground water) are all forms of geomancy. The concept derives from the historical Arabic custom of casting and reading "marks in the sand" to obtain a response to a specific question.

The four main flyways of North America follow the north-south alignment of sea coasts, mountain ranges, and river systems, and provide food and resting stops for different avian species as they make their seasonal journeys to and from their winter homes.

For thousands of years, humans depended on accurate "readings" of nature for their survival. Knowledge of the position of the stars and orientation to the cardinal directions—north, south, west, and east—held significant symbolic associations across cultures. The purpose of the geomantic arts was to assure people's health and well-being by aligning their intentions with the flow of the earth's positive energies. First detected by ancient Chinese civilization, the earth's core creates a magnetic field that can be utilized like a biological compass. Birds, butterflies, dolphins, and whales are just a few of the migratory animals that navigate by geomagnetic sense. Geomancers, and others who can perceive these hidden currents, intercede in various ways to obtain a favorable balance of energy.

To illustrate the flow and magnitude of the earth's energies, the artwork juxtaposes scientific data on ocean salinity with imagery of landscapes where land and water meet.

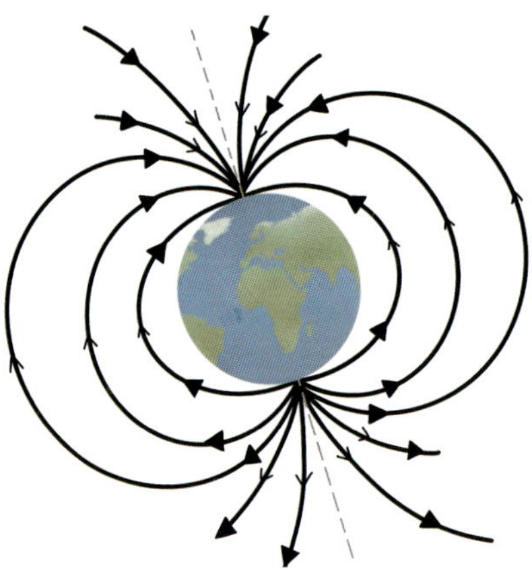

The earth's magnetic field exists between "north" and "south" poles that shift their location over time; the geological record shows that the poles have actually flipped positions in the course of the earth's history. The geomagnetic field extends into outer space and protects earth by deflecting cosmic radiation.

XI

GEOMANCY

XII

AXIS MUNDI

You are a child of the universe, no less than the trees and the stars.

Max Ehrmann, *Desiderata*, 1948

In typical tarot decks, card twelve depicts the Hanged Man. The image, representative of the concept of transition and suspension, shows a person hanging by one leg, with the other leg crossed in the form of the number four. From this position, the perspective is of a heavenly or celestial prospect. With the earth below our feet, it shows that we are grounded but can aspire to reach the stars. To reestablish a relationship with the Cosmos, we've transformed the Hanged Man into an Axis Mundi, the imagined line through the earth that connects the heavens with the underworld. Trees and mountains are natural features that often symbolize the axis mundi. Built forms, such as ziggurats, pyramids, obelisks, church spires, and many other vertically oriented elements also represent the fundamental spatial construct of centering, and exemplify significant place-making strategies of early societies.

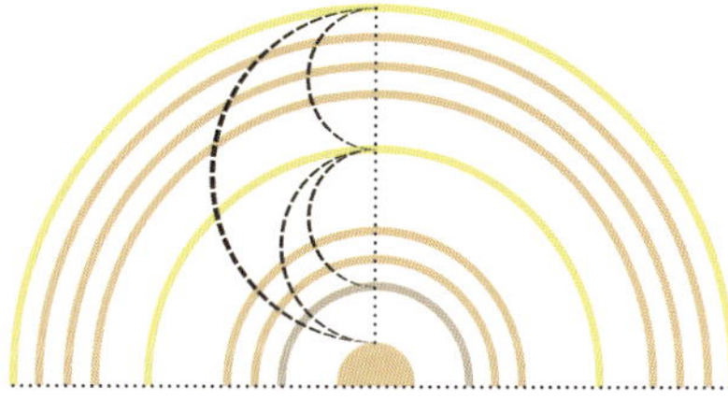

Knowing that objects in motion produce sound, the Greek mathematician Pythagoras theorized a celestial harmony caused by the rotation of the planets.

The top of the image renders the vast, unimaginable reaches of the Universe. Emerging from the middle of the illustration is the sacred pole known to the indigenous Achilpa people of Australia. This Axis Mundi is further depicted within the canopy of Yggdrasil, the "world tree" that signifies the cosmic center in Nordic mythology. These two cosmic systems are then unified with the image of a monochord. Seventeenth-century English mathematician and physician Robert Fludd theorized two worlds: the earthly microcosm and the divine macrocosm. He believed that musical forms bind the universe together in celestial harmony, and that the vibrations of a monochord could be adjusted or fine-tuned to affect frequencies throughout the Cosmos. The base of the image depicts a vision of the hidden underworld of universal consciousness.

The terraced pyramid shape of a ziggurat imitated the form of a sacred mountain. The color and material of each successive level symbolized a cosmic axis, from earth at the base to heaven above.

XII
AXIS MUNDI

XIII

METAMORPHOSIS

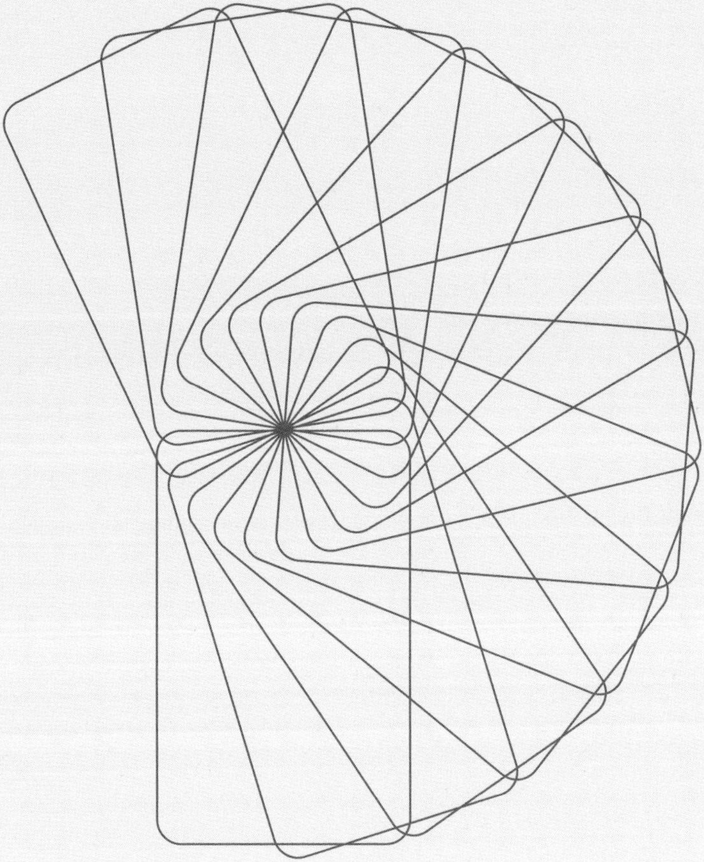

Everything teaches transition, transference, metamorphosis... We dive and reappear in new places.

Ralph Waldo Emerson, *Journals of Ralph Waldo Emerson, 1820-1824*

The thirteenth card in a conventional tarot deck is labeled Death, and when it appears in a reading one's initial reaction may be of fear and dread. On the contrary, the symbolism refers not to the end of one's life, but to a period of change and transformation. In this context, we associate the Death card with the concept of Metamorphosis. The Greek roots of the word "metamorphosis" mean to change shape or adopt a new form. In biology, we often learn about metamorphosis by studying the life stages of a butterfly—from egg, to larva, to pupa, to adult. Metamorphosis is also a geological process in which igneous or sedimentary rocks are transformed into new rocks, such as marble and slate, through the forces of heat and pressure deep below the earth's surface or where tectonic plates meet. In a geological timeframe, all rock types will change form as part of a continuous cycle.

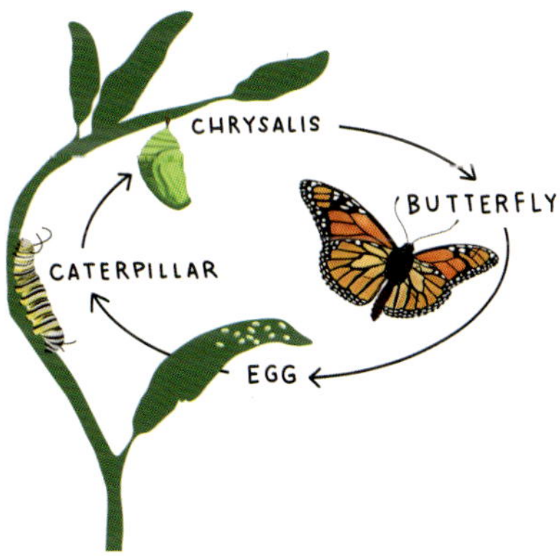

Adult butterflies lay eggs, from which caterpillars (larvae) hatch. The caterpillars grow quickly and increase in size dramatically to eventually form a chrysalis (pupa) in which development takes place. The butterfly emerges from the chrysalis fully formed, in a cycle of complete metamorphosis.

The imagery on our card depicts transformations that we experience every day—the shift between day and night, light and dark, sun and moon. The photographic process can also be considered a metamorphosis. Film is transformed by exposure to light; negatives produce positives.

Myths and social practices from cultures around the world include stories of metamorphosis. Humans turn into other life forms and adopt the identity of an animal or plant, and vice versa. The change or transformation often signifies the attainment of a power. Folklore is localized and relates to the unique spirit of a place and its people. In myths and legends of metamorphosis, the boundary between the physical world and the spiritual world is fluid and permeable.

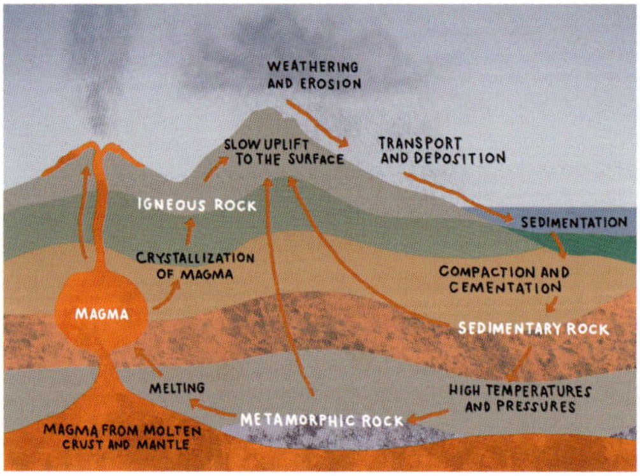

In the rock cycle, magma crystallizes to form igneous rock, which through weathering and deposition forms sedimentary rock. Dissolved minerals cause chemical reactions that change the texture of sedimentary rock to metamorphic rock, which then melts to form magma.

XIII

METAMORPHOSIS

XIV

THE TREE OF LIFE

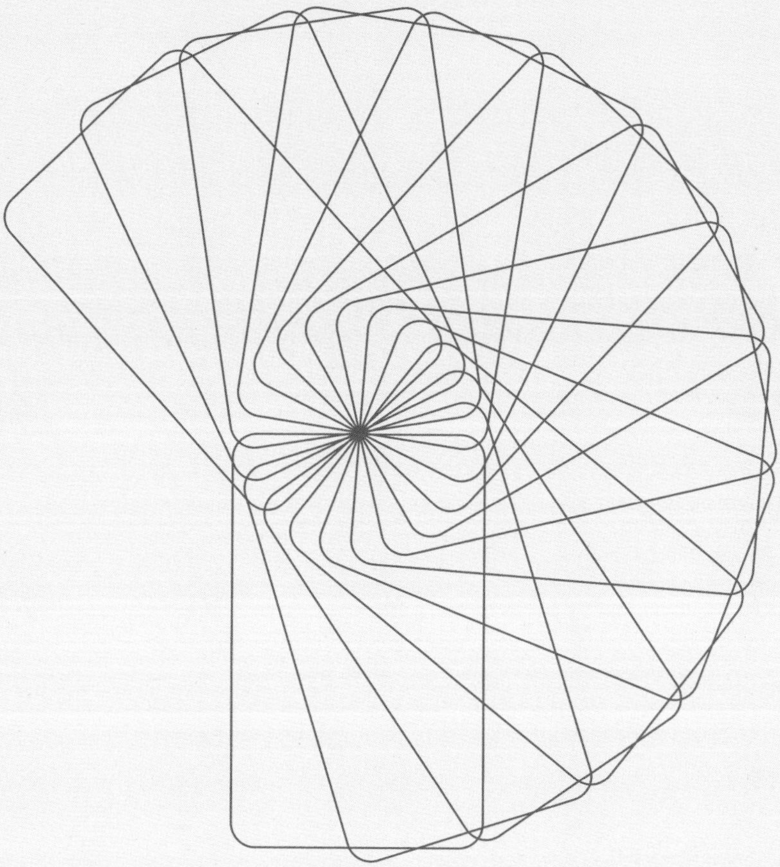

Wisdom is like a baobab tree, no one individual can embrace it.

African proverb

Our rendition of the traditional tarot card for Temperance represents the Tree of Life, an ancient symbol sacred to many cultures. This composite diagram illustrates the development of an idealized tree of knowledge, representing the connection between the earth and paradise above from a multicultural perspective. Sprouting from the canopy of the African baobab tree is the Egyptian Tree of Life, *Acacia nilotica*, or Gum Arabic. The healing and sustaining spirit of the tree pours forth from its branches into a holy urn and the waiting vessels and hands of the people. Germinating from a sacred vessel is the Persian Tree of Life, its many branches resplendent with nature's vitality.

The baobab tree *(Adamsonia grandidieri)* is one of the oldest plant forms on the planet and predates the human species by thousands of years. Native to the African

The sweet-smelling seed pods of *Acacia nilotica* traditionally have been used in dyes. Furniture and boats have been made from Acacia wood, and its resin has many practical uses. The tree's flowers, leaves, and bark have medicinal and purportedly psychoactive properties that figure in Egyptian mythology.

savanna, and capable of withstanding periods of drought by its ability to store over 4,000 gallons of water, the baobab is the symbol of life on the continent. It is an additional source of nourishment offering abundant fruit when other vegetation in the parched landscape has withered and died.

Temperance is often represented by a woman pouring water from one vessel to another. We reference this concept in the baobab's ability to function as a reservoir. Temperance also implies moderation and caution, which aligns with the critical importance of the conservation of water and natural resources.

The 100-foot-tall trees along the Avenue of the Baobobs in Madagascar are adjacent to the private Kirindy Forest reserve. Often called the "upside-down tree" the baobob became an endangered species 25 years ago.

XIV
TREE OF LIFE

XV

KOYAANISQATSI

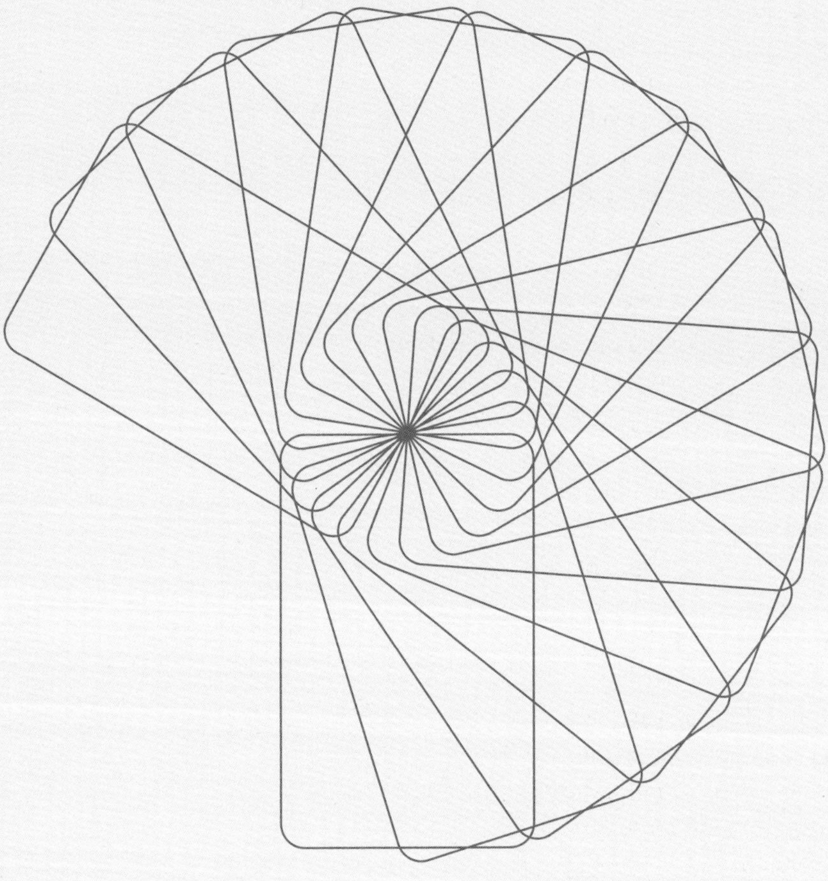

I want it said of me by those who knew me best, that I always plucked a thistle and planted a flower where I thought a flower would grow.

Abraham Lincoln (1809-1865), 16th President of the United States

The fifteenth card in a traditional tarot deck represents the Devil. We have interpreted this concept of domination by negative and limiting forces as akin to the harmful consequences wrought to the earth's biotic communities by non-indigenous species. "Koyaanisqatsi" is the Hopi word for life in turmoil, or imbalance. Provoked by this concept of dysfunction, our card represents the danger to the fragile balance of the earth's ecosystems from the uncontrolled growth of invasive plant and animal species. The abstract branching pattern of a tree is visible beneath the overlay of an urban street scene; its organic structure contrasts with the artifice of the city. Bits and pieces of currency, a sewing pattern, a language instruction flash card, and classical and folkloric symbols contribute to the sense of visual disorder.

The amount of anthropogenic mass on earth (the concrete, plastic, and metal objects made by humans from raw materials) now exceeds the total amount of biomass (the weight of all living material).

Invasive species are plants and animals that are not naturally found in a particular geographic area. As they grow and thrive in alien habitats, non-native species compete with native species for nutrients and can lead to the extinction of native species. The uncontrolled growth of invasive species can cause severe environmental problems and negative economic impacts in waterways and in wilderness areas where their populations are not monitored.

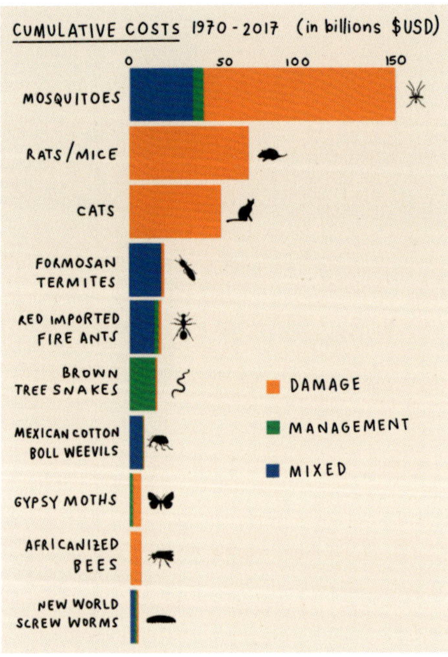

In 2021, the economic and environmental damage caused by biological invasions (the arrival, establishment, and spread of invasive species) cost the US over $120 billion.

XV

KOYAANISQATSI

XVI

ECOTONE

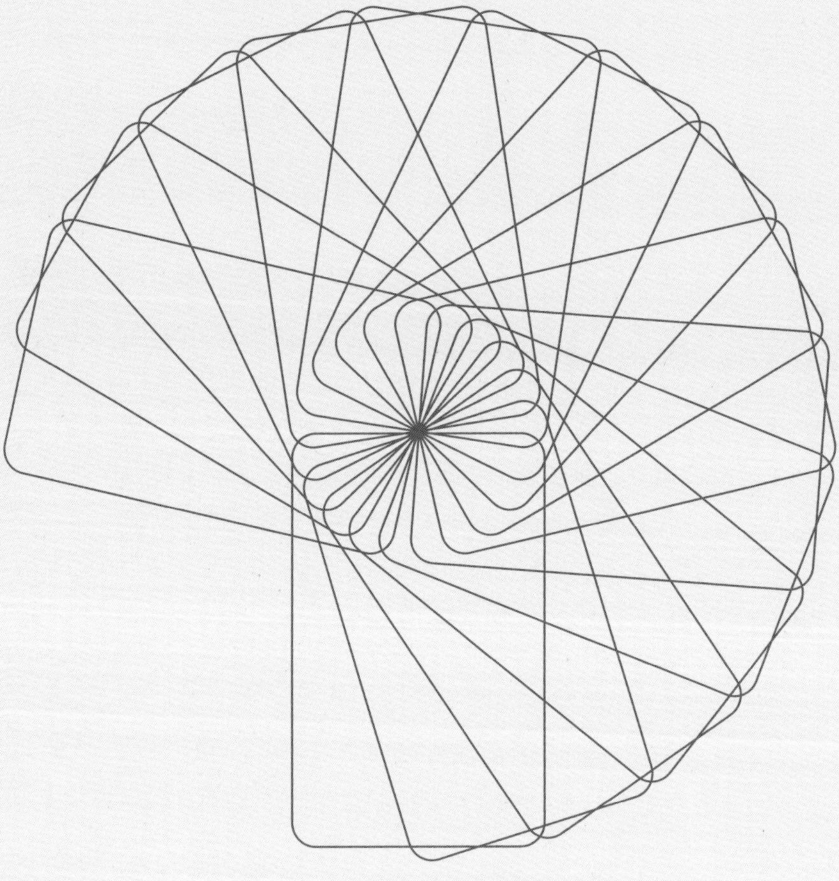

Out on the edge you see all kinds of things you can't see from the center.

Kurt Vonnegut, *Player Piano*, 1952

Traditional interpretations of the sixteenth card in a tarot deck, the Tower, represent various aspects of a prospect or lookout, including the idea of revelation and unforeseen change. We relate this concept to the omniscient ability to view the hidden workings of a natural system called an ecotone. The Tower is also a symbol of healing, restoration, and protection. Under the protection of our Tower, we envision how ecotones can be restored and healed.

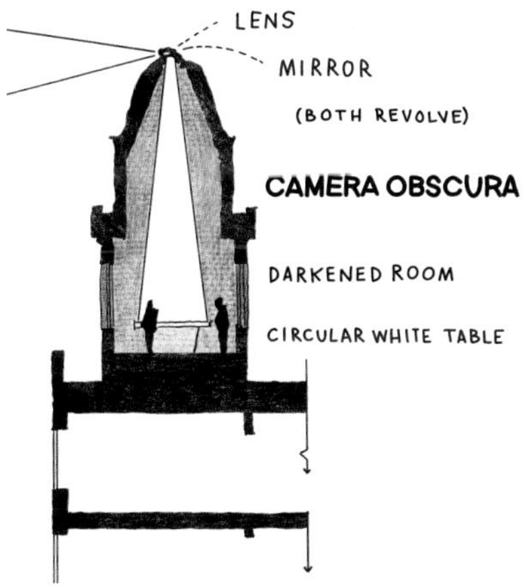

The view from Patrick Geddes's Outlook Tower (~1890) enabled this biologist-geographer to observe the patterns and processes of the landscape at a regional scale and develop theories of urban planning that link natural and social factors.

An ecotone is a zone of transition where the boundaries of different ecological communities meet and interact. It is a landscape of incredible biodiversity and abundance, critical for the conservation of many types of vegetation, and a valuable repository of trees, shrubs, flowers, grasses, and fungi. Wildlife is most active within an ecotone, as it supplies a bountiful source of food, and provides habitat and protection from predators. Animals such as deer and rabbits that require more than one type of vegetation are often termed "edge species."

At the apex of this image of this image is a watch tower, a place of observation that affords a sweeping panorama of the landscape. The complex ecotone contains a graduated layering of vegetation, from forest to deciduous and evergreen shrubs to grasses and wildflowers. Thus, the watchtower is an educational feature that serves as a platform to view the interactions of the various species that inhabit the ecotone.

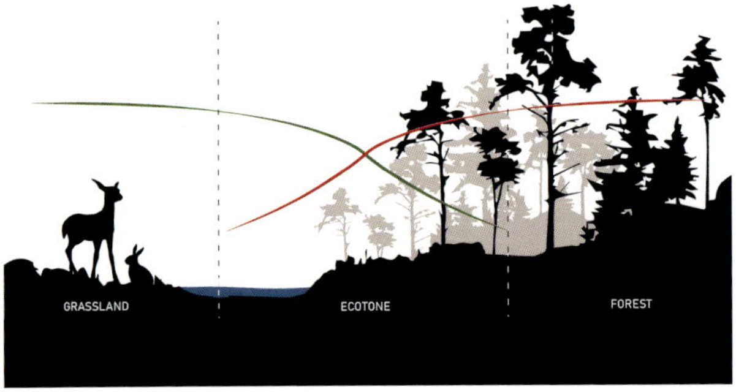

An ecotone is an area of transition from one plant community to another, such as where grassland meets forest, or where land meets sea.

XVI

ECOTONE

XVII

POLARIS

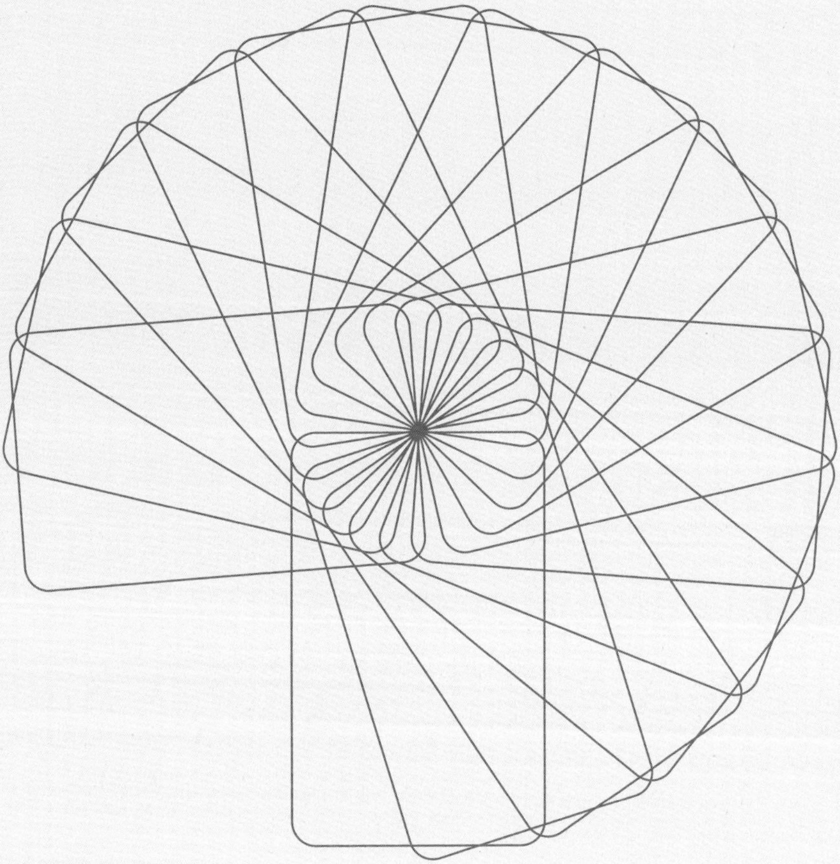

The stars are the landmarks of the universe.

Sir John Herschel (1792-1871), English astronomer

In tarot, the Star typically signifies hope and inspiration, as well as optimism and belief in a positive outcome. A shooting star is a particularly potent symbol of hope, a medium for making wishes. Watching the meteor's trail blaze briefly across the sky makes us aware of the vastness of space and time, of how we all are made of stardust ourselves. In the context of wayfinding, the stars remind us of our spiritual connection to the universe and compel us to foster our intuitive knowledge of nature's vocabulary.

Before urbanization, humans relied on their understanding of natural patterns and processes to govern their movements and activities. The stars, the sun, and the moon, as well as weather and vegetation patterns provided clues to one's position. Around the globe, Indigenous peoples historically navigated

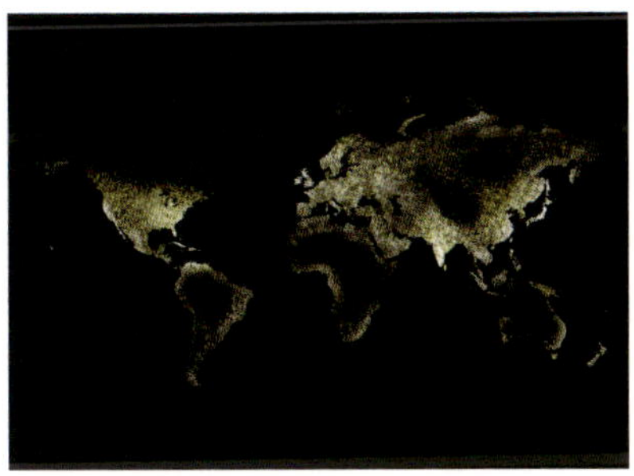

Urban light pollution affects approximately 83% of the global population; it disturbs the biorhythms of nocturnal animals, interferes with the flight patterns of migrating birds, and alters the seasonal synchronization of sea turtles.

their environments by understanding the signs and features particular to their geography; the Inuit found clues to wind direction by observing snow drifts; people of the Marshall Islands located land by observing ocean currents.

If you've ever seen a time-lapse photo of the night sky in the northern hemisphere, you'll notice circular rings around one bright star—that is Polaris, the north star, which appears stationary over the north pole. One can always orient to north by finding Polaris. Sadly, due to urban light pollution, one-third of the world's population can no longer see the Milky Way with an unaided eye.

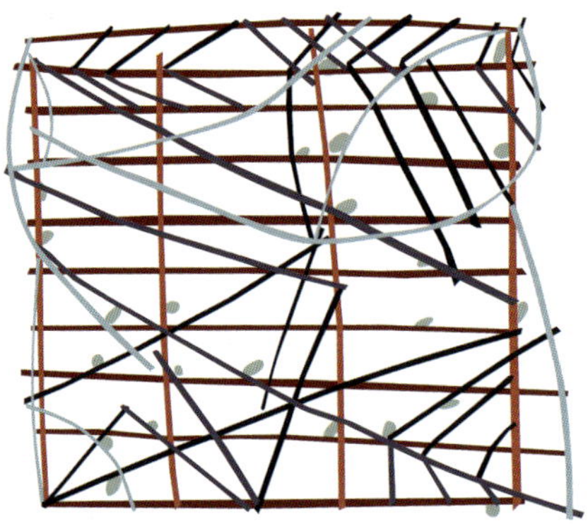

The "stick charts" traditionally made from coconut ribs and seashells by people of the Marshall Islands represent the swells and currents of the ocean relative to the position of the islands and atolls.

XVII

POLARIS

XVIII

THE MOON

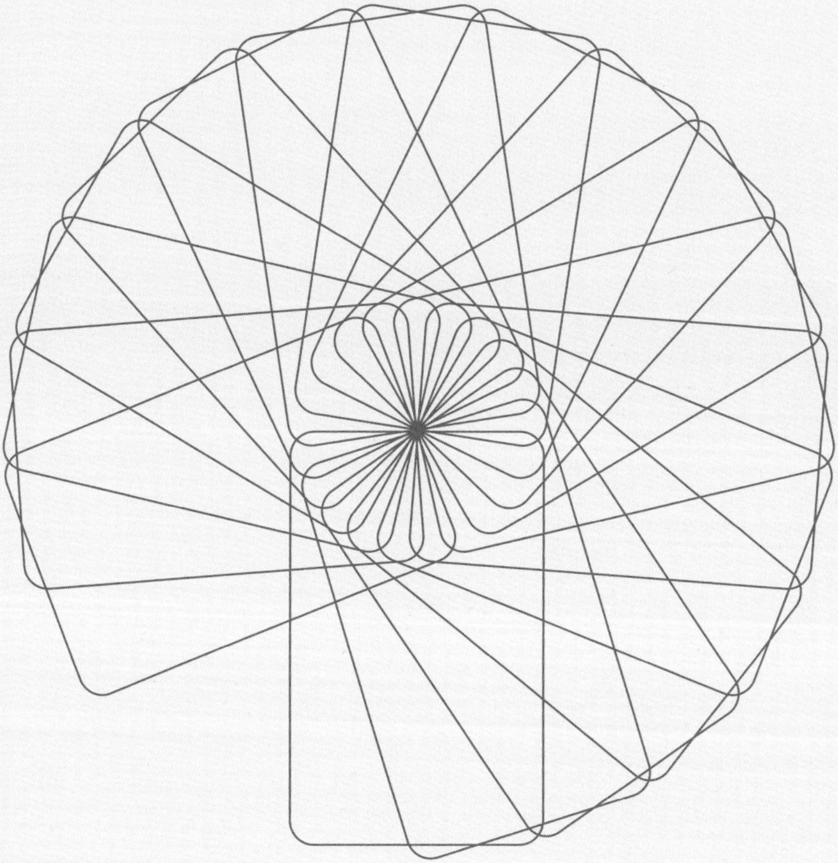

We are going to the moon. That is not very far. Man has so much farther to go within himself.

Anaïs Nin (1903-1977), Amerian writer

The Moon conjures up hidden impulses and deceptive appearances and exemplifies the vast sense of the collective subconscious. By understanding the movement of the moon and its transformational cycles we can take advantage of its creative power. The Moon is a powerful force that can move the Earth's oceans and affect the growth of plants by drawing water to the soil's surface. Knowing that the moon can impact the waters of the world, and that our human bodies are 60% water, there is no doubt that the Moon affects one's psyche, too.

The upper portion of the illustration shows the moon in its heavenly habitat. The lunar cycles are in the center of the image with their unique properties indicated. The earthly plane at the bottom depicts the flowers that bloom

Sacred Datura, or Moonflower *(Datura wrightii)*, contains narcotic and hallucinogenic alkaloids. The visionary plant has been used for millennia by Indigenous peoples of the American southwest for medicinal and ceremonial purposes.

during the full moon. Like the moon's reflection in the night sky, these species bear all white flowers. Shown here are Moon Flower, Night Blooming Daylily, Night Blooming Cerium, Evening Primrose, and Sacred Datura. In the center is a fabled fairy ring with dancers mimicking the orbit of the moon around the Earth.

Historically, peoples have used the lunar cycle to govern their planting schedules and maximize the growth of their plants. We can reeducate ourselves on how to use the power of the Moon to enhance our environment and its vegetal biomass.

Experienced gardeners know when to sow and when to reap. Plant seeds during a waxing moon to take advantage of the extra moisture drawn up in the soil; harvest during a waning moon when less water is moving through the plant.

XVIII

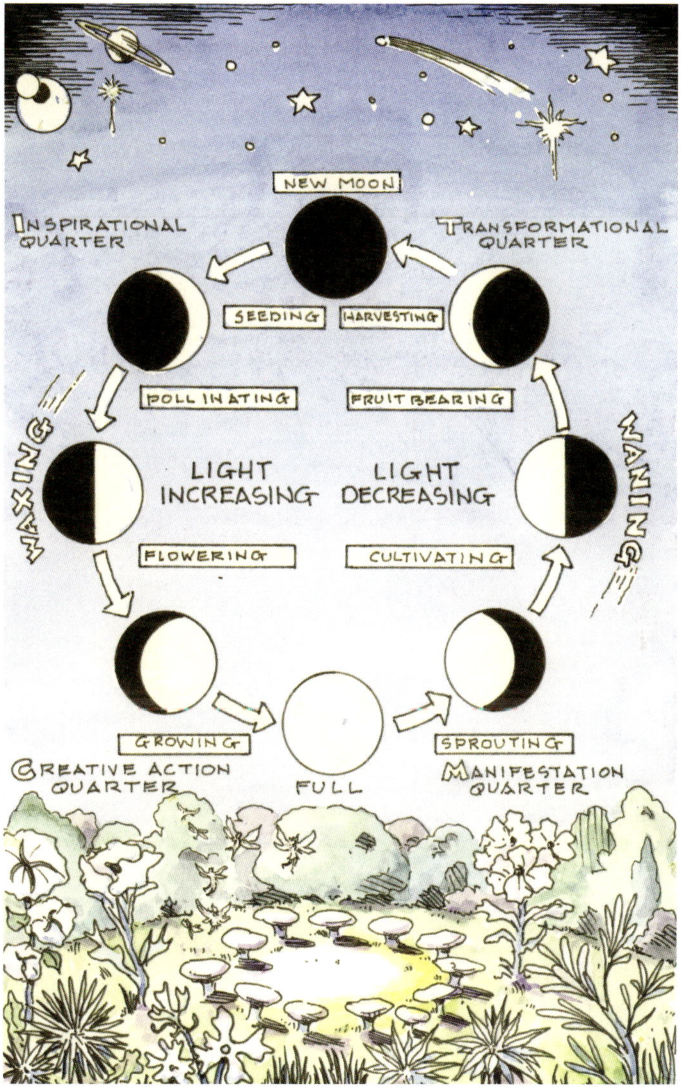

THE MOON

XIX

THE SUN

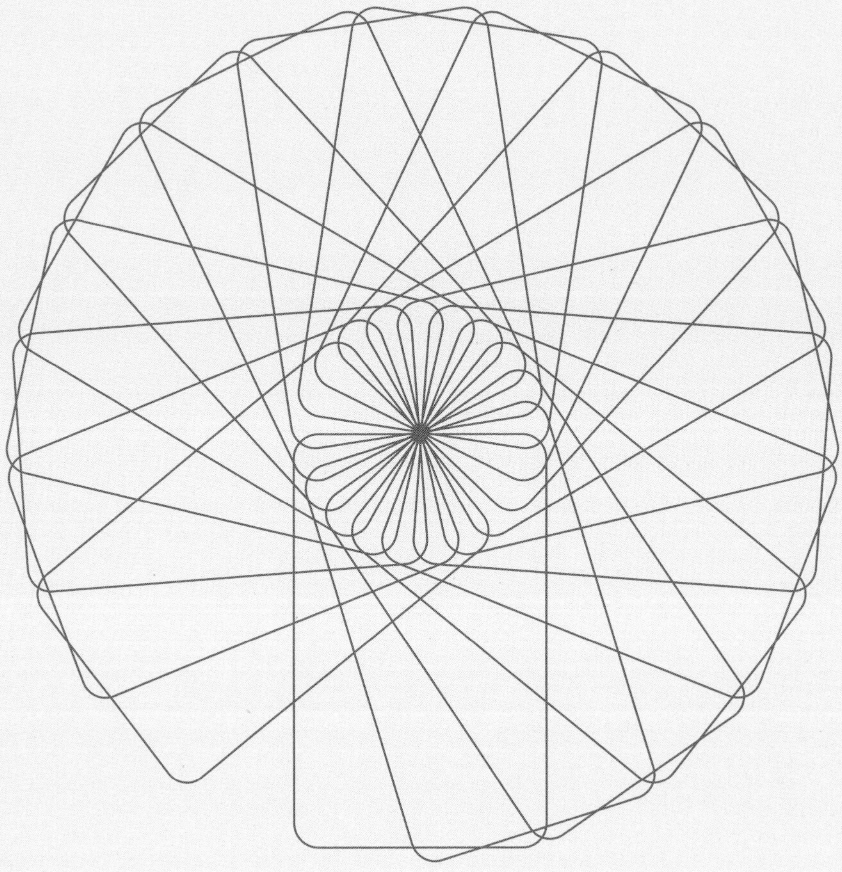

Even after all this time, the sun never says to the earth, "You owe me." Look what happens with a love like that, it lights the whole sky.

Hafiz (1350-1390), Sufi poet

The Sun is the ultimate source of all life and a vital component of every ecosystem. Through photosynthesis green plants convert sunlight into food and release oxygen in the process. The Sun provides light, heat, and energy to support the web of life on Earth. In a single day, the sun produces more energy than people consume in an entire year across the globe. Passive-energy systems, like solar power, depend on this utilitarian powerhouse rather than on external inputs of power to function. Understanding solar aspect (how the sun moves across the sky) and basic principles of thermal mass and solar gain (how different materials absorb and store heat) are attributes of traditional environmental knowledge that for centuries people have employed to create comfortable microclimates.

Passive design takes advantage of the low angle of the sun in winter to channel warmth and the high angle of the sun in summer to provide shade.

The relationship between the sun's position and seasonal patterns was critical to people whose lives were closely tied to nature. The petroglyphs created by the Anasazi people at Chaco Canyon, New Mexico, serve as solar calendars that record the longest and shortest days of the year. As did other historical Indigenous peoples, the Ancestral Puebloans of the American southwest held rituals to honor the Sun and to mark its journey across the sky. To this day winter solstice festivals continue to be held in many pueblo communities. Bonfires are lit to celebrate the return of the light and the abundant energy that the Sun exudes each day.

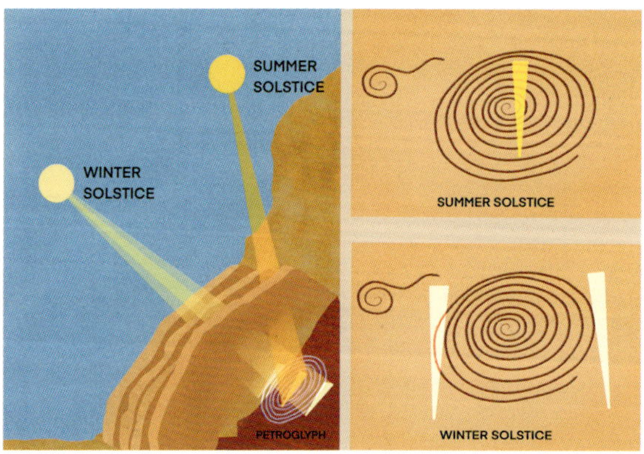

The "Sun Dagger" at Chaco Canyon casts a shadow in the center of a spiral petroglyph at summer solstice; at winter solstice the spiral is bracketed by two shadows.

XIX
THE SUN
1,392,000 km in diameter
(Not to scale)
THE SUN

XX

CLOSED LOOP

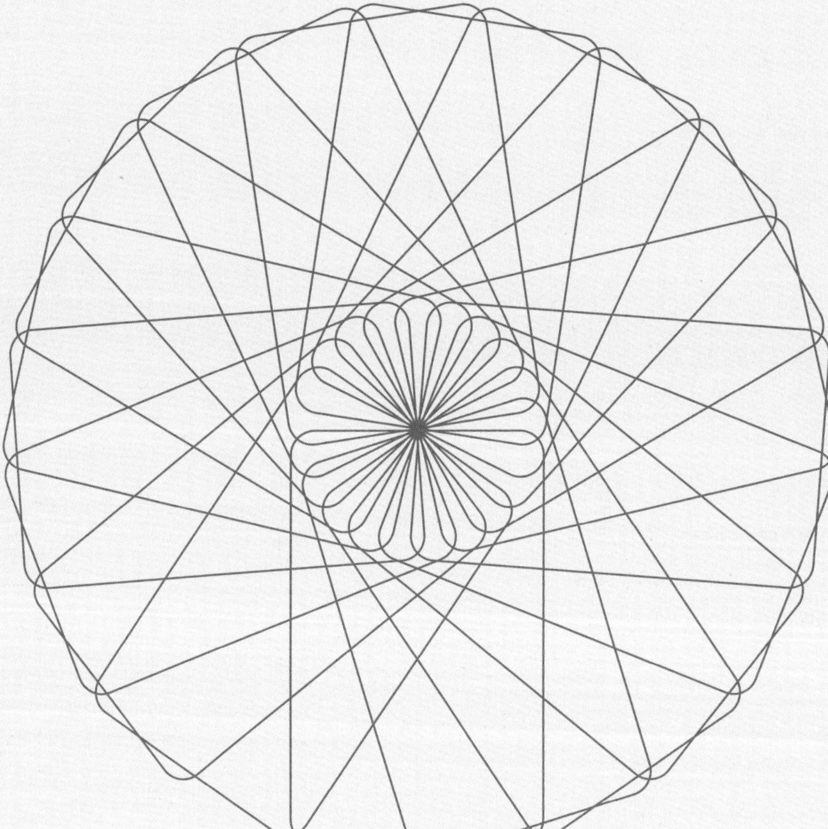

A stable forest actually is…a form of intelligence beyond that of its individual humans.

Howard Odum, *Environment, Power and Society,* 1971

Judgement is the penultimate card in a typical tarot deck. Traditional representations are related to the idea of attaining knowledge from past experiences and making reasonable assessments based on a higher level of consciousness. We illustrate this model of wise decision making in the context of landscape ecology, as a closed loop system that supports the regenerative functions of a sustainable landscape. In a closed loop, all waste is recycled and becomes a new source of food or fuel. The importance of understanding the metabolic systems of the landscape is critical to the future of a healthy planet.

Closed loops are systems in which energy inputs equal energy outputs, or losses. Ecologist Howard Odum in his groundbreaking book *Environment, Power and Society* quantified the flows of

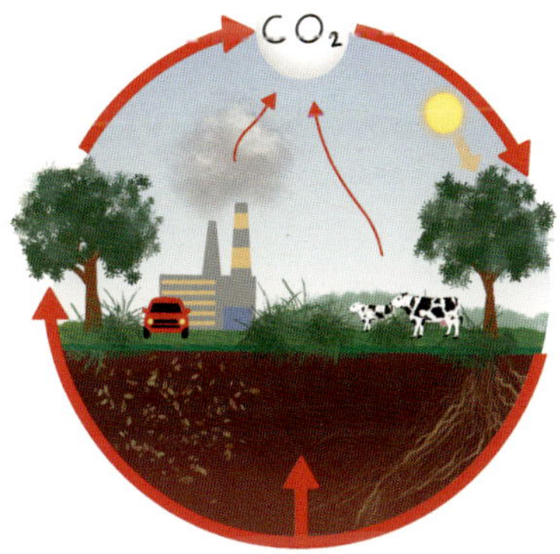

With energy inputs from the sun, atmospheric carbon dioxide is converted to organic nutrients, which, through processes of respiration, combustion, and decay, are released back into the atmosphere as carbon dioxide.

energy in a natural system and compared those systems to similar networks of power in human society. Odum's diagrams inspired our illustration of the energy transfer within a forest. The closed loop system of the climax forest is one in which all species work together to maintain stability. Carbon is stored in the trees and released into the atmosphere through cycles of growth and disturbance.

Our simplified diagram of the hidden circuits of an ecosystem shows various pathways of energy in a closed loop. The alchemical symbols for earth, air, fire, and water represent the photosynthetic process, wherein green plants convert inputs from the air (carbon dioxide) and the soil (water) into outputs of oxygen and sugars that provide a store of energy for the plant. Respiration, transpiration, and the exchange of gases and nutrients are illustrated on the right-hand side of the image.

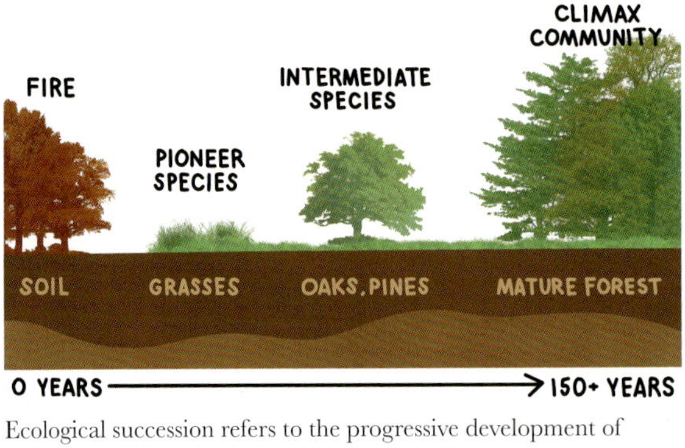

Ecological succession refers to the progressive development of a plant community from pioneer species to climax community, through processes of establishment and replacement. A climax community is the most stable and balanced.

XX
WATER VAPOR
O_2
CO_2
All ROOT-SOIL RESPIRATION
CLOSED LOOP

XXI

GENIUS LOCI

Dwelling means to gather the world...

Christian Norberg-Schulz,
***The Phenomenon of Place,* 1976**

The World is the final card of the major arcana in a traditional tarot deck; it symbolizes the successful completion of the journey begun by the Fool. Thus, our search for environmental consciousness concludes with one of the most fundamental concepts of being and dwelling in the world—the *Genius Loci* or "spirit of place." Throughout history, people of all cultures have shaped their environments according to instinctive and localized understandings of natural phenomena. In a sense, "placemaking" was a sacred act, grounded in a deep respect for the power of the earth's dynamic systems.

In the 18th century, English poet and critic Alexander Pope referenced *genius loci* as an important principle in garden and landscape design. Pope believed that a built landscape should artfully

The "blue marble" of Earth was first photographed in 1972 by astronauts aboard the Apollo 17 mission. The image had a profound impact on the environmental movement that emerged in that era.

enhance the hidden qualities and natural features of a site. In his *Epistle to the Earl of Burlington*, he famously proposed that designers "Consult the genius of the place in all." We believe that recognizing the *genius loci*—being conscious of the complexities of the environment—is the first step in creating powerful and meaningful places today.

The imagery on this card depicts the wonder and enchantment that the landscape holds for those who linger and pause to appreciate its mysteries. The World card, like its representation here as the *genius loci*, symbolizes awareness of one's connection to the greater universe. Recognizing the harmony and dynamic balance that exists between oneself and the outside world prepares us for a new journey to explore the four suits of the minor arcana.

The 18th-century English "Landscape" Garden promoted a "naturalistic" aesthetic through a vocabulary of curving lakes, hills, lawn, and tree masses.

XXI

GENIUS LOCI

MINOR ARCANA

In a typical tarot deck the four suits of the Minor Arcana—cups, swords, wands, and pentacles—represent the four elements of the universe in western cosmologies: water, air, fire, and earth, respectively. In eastern philosophies there is a cycle of five elements that constitute the universe: wood, fire, earth, metal, and water. In both systems the elements have properties and characteristics that are associated with various traits and experiences of life. Interactions between the elements can bring about change.

The four suits of our Minor Arcana blend aspects from both ideologies to define fundamental elements of sacred landscapes—water, air, wood, and earth—and their spiritual attributes. Water is the essence of life. Air supports life as well as feeds fire; fire is also a source of energy, heat, and pressure within the earth's core, so we include in this broad category stone, rock, wind, and other atmospheric phenomena. Wood manifests as tree, plant, and botanical energies. Earth is evident as topography and landform.

Within each suit we consider an individual expression as matter and as metaphor, in a progression that moves from abstraction to materiality. Wisdom of place is made manifest in examples of landscape elements, both fabled and factual. With this knowledge, a transformation—of environmental consciousness—is assured.

WATER

Without water there is no life; it is an essential natural resource and sacred element. The physical and metaphorical properties of water are symbolic of life itself. We are born from water; it is our primordial home. Water equally sustains and destroys. It is forceful in its movement and in its stillness. It is salty and sweet. Water cleanses, dissolves, dilutes, and extinguishes as well as powers, feeds, fulfills, and satisfies. It exists as solid, liquid, and vaporous matter. In mythology and religion water functions as mirror, wellspring, dwelling, source, channel, elixir, divinity, and demon.

Water is also a commodity; it is political and economic. Water infrastructure implicates the control of nature at massive scales. Water is captured, stored, and transported for a variety of agricultural, industrial, and municipal purposes. How water is accessed, used, and managed varies tremendously around the world; its distribution is not equitable. According to the United Nations, a quarter of the world's population, or two billion people, lack access to safe drinking water. The impacts of climate change on water resources are likewise significant. Sea level rise and extreme weather events have disrupted natural cycles. Innovative and sustainable technologies, better policies, and more efficient practices can reduce our water footprint. Valuing the spiritual attributes of water, as recognized in traditional environmental knowledge, will also help us prioritize its conservation.

AQUEA

Aquea is the singular, feminine form of the Latin word aqueous, meaning "watery." Water, as essential substance and as vital spirit, exists in many forms. Globally, the sacred qualities of water are often associated with female energy, representative of the womb environment, the birthing process, and motherhood.

The representation of water deities in fables and legends is naturally influenced by geography. In dry, arid climates the goddess of water brings life; she is a heroine who irrigates the land and makes it fertile. In riverine environments, the water spirit has a temporal dimension; ideas of movement and flow are significant. In coastal areas the water goddess characterizes relationships between land and sea; her power often manifests in personal or familial relationships.

In Persian folklore, **Anahita** is known as the lady of the waters, a nature deity who embodies all qualities and functions of water as matter and as myth. She is attended by four white horses symbolic of rain, wind, clouds, and hail. The Hindu goddess **Gaṅgā** is renowned as the mother of rivers. Her descent to earth from her heavenly abode brought life to the parched land. In celebration of her feat, devotees undertake a pilgrimage to bathe in the purifying waters of the mighty river Gaṅgā, which the goddess personifies. **Ma-tsu (Mazu)**, the Chinese shamaness of the sea, is believed to influence weather patterns and currents. She ensures the safety of sailors at sea and mothers during childbirth. Her legend is based on the life of a 10th-century woman who saved her brothers from drowning. **Mem loimis** represents the essence of water to the Wintu peoples of Northern California. Where water fell from the basket she had filled for her sons to bring back to her people, a spring appeared to quench the drought-stricken land. **Yemaja** is the Yoruba "orisha" or goddess of the ocean's surface. As river mother, she is also the source of all the world's waters. Our illustration aims to synthesize the power and beauty of all the divine feminine water spirits.

I

AQUEA

MERFOLK

Merfolk are typically described as being half fish and half human. From the waist up they have the body of a human and from the waist down the body of a fish with a flexible tailfin. They inhabit the seas but can also live in fresh water; remarkably, over the centuries they have been observed and recorded in almost every sea on the planet.

In mythology, the mermaid is said to represent the sacred feminine. The earliest known mermaid legend begins in Assyria in the first century BCE. The beautiful fertility goddess Atargatis dove into a lake taking on the form of a fish, but the gods would not allow her to entirely give up her beauty, so she was compelled to keep her human upper body. Merfolk symbolize awareness and insight by having heightened consciousness of the aquatic world they inhabit.

Almost every culture in the world has a belief in merfolk. Perhaps this phenomenon of the universal belief in merfolk can be found in our DNA, as our ancestors evolved out of the sea thousands of millennia ago. We are thought to have evolved from the Aquatic Tetrapods over 350 million years ago when we incrementally moved onto land.

The 17th-century alchemical text *Clavis Artis* represents an intertwined mermaid holding a moon and a merman holding a sun within a flask sprouting a flower. For the earth to flower we need to decipher this universal belief in merfolk and reimagine our ancestral aquatic origins.

II
MERFOLK

NAIADS

The term *naiad* originates from the Greek word for flow. Naiads are the deities of flowing water in Greek mythology. They protect and have dominion over the sources of freshwater that sustain communities and are classified relative to their abode: the Crinaeae dwell in fountains, the Limnades in lakes, the Pegaeae in springs, the Potameides in rivers, and the Eleionomae in marshes. As water spirits, they nourish all forms of life and are revered as guardians and healers. A naiad's wellbeing corresponds to the health and vigor of the water source; if the supply dries up, she will perish. The same is true of human settlements. As freshwater supplies decline worldwide due to climate change, water scarcity will increasingly endanger more of the world's populations. Throughout history, the availability of fresh water has been the primary criteria for the development of civilization. Myths often tell of a mortal king or god founding a city by marrying a naiad. Today, many place names derive from the naiad or water spirit identified with a specific location. For example, the Seine River in France is named after the Celtic goddess Sequana.

A knowledge of place is embedded in the sacred practices and restorative rituals that occur around bodies of water. Many Indigenous peoples view water as a gift rather than a resource, and their traditional management techniques reflect their spiritual beliefs. Stories and cautionary tales about the need to respect and honor the spirits of flowing water are passed down through generations to discourage actions that might contaminate or pollute the source. Water is protected and conserved with a collective consciousness of spiritual ecology, of how waterways, and the ways of water, connect people to place.

III

NAIADS

THE RAIN DANCE

The Rain Dance is a weather modification ritual that attempts to bring rain. They are performed by Indigenous peoples in Africa, China, Europe, and North America. The ceremonial dances performed by native peoples in the American Southwestern, in particular the Navajo and Hopi, are recognized worldwide, and critical to a region prone to drought. Rain dances are performed during the driest month of the year, usually in late August, to summon the spirits and cleanse the earth with rain.

The steps of the ritual are very intricate involving both men and women standing in separate lines and making a zigzag pattern. This zigzag form is invoked because it imitates the patterns of lightning. The Hopi dancers circle the plaza producing a form of climatic energy, performing the ritual with snakes in their mouths. Special ceremonial clothing decorated with feathers and turquoise is worn for this dance to symbolize wind and rain. As the participants dance, they are reenacting the process of precipitation, becoming like the rain.

With the current epidemic of droughts around the world, it might be time to integrate the rain dance into modern society—a means to engage and raise awareness of the natural rhythms of climate and cycles of weather.

IV
THE RAIN DANCE

FOG CATCHERS

Fog forms when air at the earth's surface falls below the dew point. Water vapor condenses into miniscule droplets that are suspended in the air. What was invisible, becomes visible. Fog dissipates when the air warms up.

The capacity of fog to mysteriously obscure and shroud the landscape is at the base of much folkore, often symbolizing uncertainty and otherworldliness. In Irish myth, *féth fiad*a is the "druid's mist" or invisibility cloak that conceals the identity of spiritual beings to mortals. In Norse mythology, *Niflheim*, the foggy underworld of cold and ice, is one of the nine realms that form the cosmos. "Mist" or "cloud" is also identified in ancient Nordic poetry as one of the Valkyries or female warriors who ride through air and over water.

One of the foggiest places on earth is also one of the driest: the Atacama Desert in Chile. Fog originates on the coast of the Pacific Ocean and is carried by the wind about two and a half miles inland toward the Andes mountains. The fog, known locally as "camanchaca" is harvested with nets called *atrapanieblas* to supply water for the community primarily for agricultural use. Water drips from the tightly woven nets into a trough below and is collected in a tank or vessel. A 25-foot by 25-foot net can produce about 140 gallons per day. With efficient management and maintenance, fog catchers have the potential to provide drinking water in places with similar environmental conditions.

V

FOG CATCHERS

WATER JARS

"Reading" a water jar is a form of hydromancy, or water divination—an ancient technique dating back to the second century but still practiced today. For the adept, water scrying can be used to receive prophecies and revelations, or gain insight. Through the study and interpretation of the shapes and flows of a body of water, it is possible to detect significant information and activate visions. Reading a jar of water from a specific location can be an aid for channeling mystical insight between the reader and the site.

To practice the art of reading a water jar, find a medium-sized clear glass jar with a lid. Either you or someone associated with the specific location you want to read should collect a sample of water from the site. The collection of the water can take on special significance by metaphysically connecting one to a location. Find a quiet, semi-darkened room in which to read the water. Close your eyes and concentrate on what you want to learn from the reading; let your subconscious wander, free associate, and try to attain a trance state. Watch the images that begin to appear in the water as they change and evolve. Record your impressions and insights. The French astrologer Nostradamus received many of his predictions from gazing into a bowl of water. Leonardo da Vinci believed that water was to the world as blood was to the body. Just as the blood flowing through our veins supports our life, the life-giving water flowing across the earth sustains our planet.

VI

WATER JARS

CISTERNS

The ability to capture and store rainwater is essential in dry climates where groundwater is not available. Cisterns represent an ancient technology for harvesting rainwater that assured survival in arid regions where springs and wells do not exist. A cistern is a water storage tank or vessel typically located underground that acts like a reservoir. Historically made of stone or plaster, archeologists have uncovered cisterns below dwellings in the Middle East that date from the Neolithic age.

One of the oldest cisterns in Rome functioned for nearly 1000 years, from the 4th-century BCE to the 6th-century CE. It supplied a fountain dedicated to the nymph, Anna Perenna, whose name comes from the Latin for perennial stream, *amnis perennis*. Objects and coins found in the cistern represent offerings to the deity, indicating that it was an important sacred site. Similarly, the Basilica Cistern in Istanbul was built in the 6th century nearby the Hagia Sophia and functioned for centuries to supply fresh water for the palace. With a capacity of 100,000 tons, it is the largest covered cistern in the world, containing a grid structure of over 300 marble columns. The ancient wisdom of using cisterns to capture runoff from hillsides and roof structures was also common practice in Maya and Olmec cultures. At Xochicalco, "the place of the flower house," there is evidence that water was distributed in terra cotta pipes from a cistern that was built in the 8th century.

"Smart" cisterns are being built today in drought-prone areas for irrigation, toilet flushing, and firefighting purposes. They also help to keep polluted runoff from reaching waterways via storm sewers. A surge in stormwater discharge can cause catastrophic flooding and destroy habitats, and, left untreated, polluted runoff threatens the availability of clean drinking water. Capturing, filtering, and storing rainwater in cisterns is one step toward a sustainable future.

VII

CISTERNS

THE NILOMETER

Historically, the health and welfare of a community was emphatically connected to the ebb and flow of water: too much water and the community drowns; too little water and the community starves. Before our complex weather prediction systems, the awareness of the flow of water was extremely important to the health or fate of a community, and daily observation of the movement of water helped prepare for calamity or wellbeing.

The Nilometer originated in ancient Egypt; Romans also developed similar devices. The Egyptian nilometer is a stone structure built on the banks of the river that measures the height of the water as well as the strength and turbidity of the water; it might take the form of a hollow column, a stepped bank, or a deep well attached to the river through a culvert.

The nilometer on Roda Island in Cairo was built in 861 CE by the Muslim astronomer Alfraganus. During this era only priests and rulers were allowed to observe and measure the water most likely as a way to control the sacred knowledge. The water levels were marked off in cubits (a measurement system based on human proportions), representing a gradient of conditions from Disaster and Abundance, to Security and Happiness, and finally to Suffering and Hunger.

VIII

THE NILOMETER

SPRINGS

A natural spring occurs where water from an underground source (such as an aquifer or water table) reaches the surface of the earth. No wonder springs are magical places; they represent the completion of a journey from the dark recesses of the earth to the light of day. The journey may be brief or extend over millennia depending on the depth of the groundwater. The quality and quantity of spring water is determined by many factors that are specific to a site including rock and soil structure, temperature, and volume. So, too, are the spirits of a spring dependent on local conditions.

In addition to the presumed health benefits of bathing in hot springs and drinking mineral water from popular sources, such as Evian, Perrier, and San Pellegrino, springs also provide refuge for wildlife species that are particularly sensitive to fluctuations in climate. Springs are sanctuaries and indicators of ecosystem health. Once an aquifer is depleted, by pumping out groundwater or through activities such as mining and deforestation, it is gone forever and cannot be restored.

As portals or windows between interior and exterior worlds, springs are thought to have sacred and healing properties. Throughout time people have left offerings and ex-votos around springs to draw from the power of place. Springs are also associated with inspiration and creativity.

In Greek myth, the home of the Muses was created where the hoof of the winged horse Pegasus struck the ground. (The name Pegasus comes from the Greek word *pēgē*, meaning spring.) Similarly, in Islamic tradition, water arose in places where the foot of the infant Isma'il (as well as the angel Jibra'il) touched the ground. In China, legend has it that the inexhaustible springs of Laoshan were formed where shards from a magic bowl tossed against the cliff by the villager Wang Quan hit the ground. Likewise, the word *quan* means spring in Chinese.

IX
SPRINGS

VERNAL POOLS

Vernal pools are small ephemeral wetland habitats with non-porous soils that form in natural depressions of the landscape to hold seasonal water. These shallow depressions fill up with rain or melted snow in fall or spring and usually evaporate by midsummer. They are not connected to typical water sources such as streams and rivers because there is no inlet or outlet for flow. Interestingly, they always appear in the same location but will vary in size.

Specific species of plants and animals that rely on vernal pools are uniquely adapted to both aquatic and terrestrial habitats. Obligate species are flora and fauna that depend on a particular place and condition to breed. Some of the obligate species that are associated with vernal pools are the marbled salamander, spotted salamander, wood frog, and the appropriately named fairy shrimp. Eighty-five percent of amphibians will return to the same pool in which they were born to breed. Additionally, vernal pools host vegetation species that are specifically adapted to this unique environment. Most vernal pools are considered drought tolerant landscapes and have between 15-25 types of plants that create shade and influence water levels, habitat, shelter, and egg-laying sites.

A harbinger of spring, vernal pools are magical, visual proof of the metamorphosis, or rebirth of nature. The cracked, parched earth of the vernal pool is pregnant with invisible life forms waiting for the right moment to reemerge. They illustrate the latent creative power of the earth by making us aware of the cycles of the seasons.

X

VERNAL POOLS

RUNNELS

A runnel is a shallow, narrow channel of water. Runnels can carve themselves naturally into tidal areas and wetlands or be constructed to move water across a landscape for a variety of functional and aesthetic purposes. The line and path of a runnel can have a strong impact, visually and ecologically, on the patterning of the ground plane.

Across the Earth, agricultural patterns are determined by the layout of irrigation canals; the rectilinear form of many historical gardens imitated these utilitarian geometries. In arid regions of the middle east and western Asia, underground channels called *qanats* were built to bring water by gravity flow from the hills to the settlements. Regularly spaced circular vents visible on the desert floor trace the line of the aqueduct below.

Runnels can also have symbolic significance. In ancient Persian *chahar-bagh* gardens, runnels representing the four rivers of paradise mentioned in the Qur'an divided the garden into quadrants with a central basin at their intersection. Often lined with blue tiles, the runnels created the sense of a lush oasis in a dry climate, cooling the air and calming the mind with the gentle flow of water.

Runnels incised in the stone floors of many Chinese garden pavilions mimic the natural meander of a stream renowned in history as the site of the famous poetry contest at Lanting. During the traditional Spring Purification Festival, people would ceremoniously bathe in streams to wash off the bad spirits of winter. Legend tells of the fourth century poet and calligrapher Wang Xizhi who hosted a festival "after party." He floated wine cups downstream and invited scholars to compose a poem as a cup reached them, or else drink the wine. By the end of the day, thirty-seven poems were written, with Wang Xizhi penning his famous *Preface to the Orchid Pavilion Gathering*, an important calligraphic masterwork of art history.

XI

RUNNELS

STEP WELLS

Step wells were rudimentary well-like structures developed for easy water access in periods of drought and other fluctuations in water availability. The long corridors of stone steps leading down to a water table originated in Western India between the 7th and 9th centuries and can be found in other parts of India, Pakistan, Indonesia, and surrounding arid regions. Historically, step wells also functioned as community gathering places as well as reservoirs. The subterranean character of the well provides a cool microclimate for leisure on hot summer days. Over time the structures were crafted into geometrically precise architectural masterpieces; the styles vary by region and time period.

Step wells are used for drinking, washing, bathing, and crop irrigation. In addition to being utilitarian, the wells had social, cultural, and religious significance; they were a place to pray, worship, and leave gifts to the goddess of the well. Water is identified in Indian culture as a purifying and renewing element; because of water's sacred qualities, step wells were often elaborately embellished like temples, and sometimes constructed near temples.

In India, thousands of step wells were built over hundreds of years, often commissioned by the wealthy, royal, and powerful—those who could afford such feats of civil engineering. When the British colonized India in the 19th century, step wells were deemed unsanitary, and their use diminished. With modernization of water delivery systems and falling water tables, many step wells were abandoned, destroyed, or filled.

XII

STEP WELLS

GROTTOES

A grotto is a cave-like recess or niche in an earthen wall or hillside customarily marking the site of a natural spring. As a place where a subterranean force surfaces, a grotto is symbolic of both earth and water elements—the shelter and refuge of the dark and mysterious cave, combined with the inspiring and life-giving spirit of a spring. In Greek myth, grottoes were revered as the sacred dwelling places of the Naiads; as spaces of transformation and reflection they remain spiritually significant landscapes within many world religions today.

Grottoes can be naturally occurring or human made. Ovid describes the bath of Diana as a grotto "wrought by no artist's hand, but Nature." Artificial grottoes were common features in Italian Renaissance gardens and 18th-century English gardens, designed to evoke classical themes and allegories of nature. Decorated with stones, river rocks, and shells, at a time when the study of natural history was gaining popularity, they recreated the drama and intrigue of entering the earth, and celebrated the spring as a source of power and abundance.

In addition to their narrative content, grottoes also serve an ecological purpose. They afford escape from the summer heat by taking advantage of the insulating capacity of the earth. They function to moderate a microclimate by adding moisture to the air, reducing temperatures, and providing psychological cooling.

Ovid. Miller, F. J. & Goold, G. P. (1984). *Metamorphoses*. Cambridge, Mass: Harvard University Press.

XIII
GROTTOES

NYMPHAEUMS

The nymphaeum, or water theater, was a common feature of the Italian Renaissance garden. They were inspired by the ancient Roman structures constructed to placate and worship the nymphs, to ensure that the springs would continue to flow. In mythology, nymphs were lower ranking female divinities that were the spirits and protectors of nature, and very important in the belief system surrounding the natural world. Naiads were a specific species of water nymph identified with the flowing water of rivers, wells, and springs. Nymphs could gift humans with certain powers, such as prophecy, and are noted to have nurtured many Olympian gods when they were young.

The structure of the nymphaeum can be a secluded niche built into a terrace or a semi-circular enclosure resembling a theater, sometimes several stories high. These structures, often considered sacred spaces, contained grottoes and springs where nymphs and other water deities were believed to live. Imagine a place where the oracles of the water nymphs are delivered in a theatrical display—aquatic actors reciting their oracles through the sound of water. The nymphaeum is a setting where humans are allowed to enter their inner sanctum.

With the mounting desecration of water bodies worldwide, humans must slow down and reactivate the power of the water nymph. Learning to listen to the hidden meanings expressed through the rhythmic sound of water playing in the theater can help us respect its oracular power and save the aquatic world.

XIV

NYMPHAEUMS

AIR

Air is the force and rhythm of life. From our first breath to our last, we cycle oxygen through our bodies, taking in the energy and spirit of air and releasing it. People often associate air with the idea of endless possibilities, with freedom, with intellect—the place where our thoughts and dreams "take flight." We gaze at the stars and see figures in the constellations; our heads are "in the clouds." We think of air as an invisible substance, yet we "see" air when it's cloudy, we "feel" air when it's windy. Air carries sound and scent. Change rides in on the wind.

Air is elemental. Along with Water, Fire, and Earth, it represents one of the four substances that were thought to comprise all of nature in Western culture. At the base of Eastern philosophies is the dynamic cycle of creation and destruction embodied by Five Elements: Wood, Fire, Earth, Metal, and Water. Air is not specifically identified in the Five Elements tradition but is an integral component of them all. In our suit of Air we include manifestations of Fire as well as Stone, considering that combustion requires oxygen, and that rocks are formed by heat, pressure, and weathering. Additionally, Air and Fire are both active elements, traditionally associated with masculine energies.

Air upholds life; yet, alarmingly, according to the World Health Organization 99% of the world's population breathes air that exceeds acceptable levels for particulate matter, making air pollution a major public health hazard particularly for people living in low-income countries. Since the late 19th century, the level of greenhouse gasses (carbon dioxide and methane) in the atmosphere has soared due to the burning of fossil fuels. Globally, the United States, China, and Russia produce the largest amount of CO2. Renewable energy sources will help reduce air pollution and mitigate the effects of climate change; renewing our awareness of the sanctity of air is an essential first step.

CULTURAL BURNING

Cultural burning is the activation of controlled fires set by Indigenous peoples following traditional beliefs and knowledge systems. This tradition provides important wisdom about how to conduct prescribed burns today. For thousands of years, the Aboriginal people of Australia have been following an ancient practice of using fire to revitalize the landscape. Native stewards across the western United States routinely tended their landscapes through controlled burning to remove excess vegetation, ground cover, and dead trees. The Indigenous peoples of California describe their controlled burns as *good fires*. Good fire eliminates the dying and dead plants and invasive species. Fire is a tool to bring back new life, so water doesn't run off but is retained in the vegetation. In the mid-1800s, cultural burning was outlawed and even criminalized and replaced with practices of fire suppression.

To conduct a cultural burn each member of the team carries a bundle of lit grass to the ground that is to be burned. Individuals spread out and set fire to small, evenly-spaced tufts of grass, creating a slow-moving fire. Following behind, another group uses long sticks to spread and direct the fire in a controlled manner.

Traditional ecological knowledge and place-based understanding of nature underlies native practices regarding controlled burning. Creation stories such as ones involving Coyote and other animals in relationship with fire help guide current tribal burning practices. In the American west, cultural burns are crucial to keeping watersheds healthy and to restoring landscapes ravaged by drought due to climate change. When *good fire* is used on the land, the water comes back and stays.

I

CULTURAL BURNING

LIGHTNING

Physically and metaphorically, lightning strikes. Its power to illuminate, spark, and ignite, to inspire and destroy—in a flash—makes it a universal subject of awe and fear, and source of myth. Lightning is Zeus's weapon; the thunderbolt is Indra's. Thor triggered thunderstorms with a blow from his hammer. Lightning symbolizes different things to different peoples around the world, yet it is commonly respected as a powerful force that both heals and damages. Lightning starts wildfires that burn forests and grasslands yet it brings rain to nourish plants and crops. These dualities are embodied by Raijin, the Shinto god of lightning; by Impundulu, the lightning bird of South Africa; and by the Thunderbird, who is sacred to many Indigenous peoples of North America.

Lightning is the transfer of static electricity. It occurs when a negative charge at the base of a cloud meets the positive charge of an object on the ground. The current travels with rapid speed and generates enormous heat which produces the peal of thunder. Lightning strikes the earth millions of times each day, working to balance the planet's electrical field. Through a chemical process in the atmosphere, lightning also produces nitrates (an ingredient in fertilizer) that then fall to the earth with rain and are absorbed by a plant's roots.

Experts predict that thunderstorms will intensify with global warming; lightning will increase by more than 10% for each 1°C rise in temperature. The Democratic Republic of the Congo experiences the most lightning anywhere on earth. The highest concentration of persistent lightning occurs around Lake Maracaibo in Venezuela. The phenomenon is so reliable that it has been used for centuries as a wayfinding aid.

II

LIGHTNING

THE EQUINOX & SOLSTICE

Throughout history Indigenous cultures have sought the synchronization and integration of the solar and lunar cycles into their lives and architecture. From approximately 900 to 1130 CE, Chacoan society, a prehistoric Pueblo culture, constructed numerous structures throughout the arid San Juan Basin of northwestern New Mexico. Pueblo Bonito is the largest archaeological site from this era, consisting of hundreds of adjacent rooms above and below ground. Twelve of the fourteen major Chacoan buildings are oriented to the Equinox and Solstice. Their site plans, architecture, and religious structures are derived from a relationship to the cycles of the sun and moon, and are based on solar and lunar cosmology. For example, at Pueblo Bonito, the equinox sun rises and sets almost perfectly in line with the western half of the south wall of the complex. The central north-south meridian wall, which bisects the structure, produces no shadow at noon throughout the year.

In Turkey, the ancient structures at Karahan Tepe that were discovered in the Tek Tek Mountains National Park are also believed to have a sacred solar function. A unique carved sculpture with the face of a goddess protrudes from the western wall of this circular structure. On the southeast edge of the pit, a portal hole leads out to the main enclosure. On the winter solstice light will enter the chamber, first illuminating the serpentine neck, then the cheek, then move toward the mouth, which in some prehistoric traditions is considered the divine source. As the Sun completes its arc, it bathes the goddess's face in total light. Karahan Tepe was believed to be a place of regeneration and healing.

III

THE EQUINOX & SOLSTICE

WIND ROSE

Wind is air in motion, a powerful agent of change, invested with spiritual meaning and capable of affecting mind, body, and soul. Wind is considered the breath of the Earth by many Indigenous peoples of North America. In Māori culture, the four winds are believed to support the sky. Wind is personified by various deities such as Grandmother Yeongdeung, the Korean goddess who visits earth each spring to assure favorable winds for the fishing community, and Vayu, the Hindu god of wind and bestower of *prana* or breath.

Winds can be as violent as a cyclone or as pleasant as a summer breeze. In many parts of the world, wind embodies the properties of the four cardinal directions, the four elements, the four seasons, and the four temperaments. The specific qualities and characteristics of wind—its temperature, humidity, force, and direction—may relate to particular physical and emotional states. Relentless wind can make us anxious; still air can cause "the doldrums."

In numerous parts of the world, winds are named according to where they originate, and they embody attributes unique to that source. Throughout time, wind has been a primary means of orientation. A wind "rose" is a circular diagram divided by segments that, to early cartographers, resembled the form of a flower. The modern wind rose is a scientific graphic that indicates the direction, speed and frequency of wind at a particular time and place. The data is used by pilots, sailors, city planners, architects, farmers, and anyone concerned with weather patterns and microclimate design. On today's maps, the wind rose has been replaced by the compass rose, essentially erasing any references to the geographical and spiritual associations of wind.

IV

WIND ROSE

STANDING STONES

The Carnac alignment in Brittany is the largest collection of standing stones in the world; its function remains one of the great unsolved mysteries. Erected during the Neolithic period sometime between 4500 and 3300 BCE, there are some 3,000 *menhirs* (or standing stones) in all. The Carnac alignments include three major stone groupings: Ménec, Kermario, and Kerlescan. The Ménec alignments are configured in eleven long rows stretching nearly three-quarters of a mile, in an area as wide as a football field. A little further east is the fan like design of the Kermario alignment, which consists of more than one thousand stones aligned in ten rows nearly a mile long. To the east of both of these groupings is the smaller Kerlescan alignment, which is laid out in thirteen lines about one-half mile long. In this alignment the stones vary in height from thirteen to three feet high.

The experience of walking through these continuous rows of standing stone alignments is transformative. Row upon row, the perspective seems infinite as the strange stones cast ominous shadows. One loses their sense of orientation as the stones take on anthropomorphic characteristics.

Many strange myths are associated with these alignments. Some legends attribute the creation of the stones to Merlin, who turned a Roman legion into megaliths. Another theory proposes that the stones might have functioned as an astronomical observatory, agricultural calendar, or even burial markers. In any event, they are a powerful and mystifying experience.

V

STANDING STONES

SCENT

Scent is a powerful tonic, capable of triggering emotions and memories of place and time. Fragrance and aroma influence our actions and behaviors, both intentional and involuntary. We are attracted by certain smells and repulsed by others. Animals use scent as a defense mechanism. Our ability to discriminate between different scents was critical to the survival of our human species, helping us recognize food, danger, and even mates. The loss of one's sense of smell was a dreadful symptom of the COVID-19 virus.

Scent is illusive and magical. It is invisible, drifting through the air, often remaining long after its source is gone. Nefertem was the Egyptian god of scent. He is depicted wearing a headpiece of blue lotus, symbolic of rebirth. He spread fragrance in his wake and caused flowers to bloom. Throughout time, scent has been a factor in religious rituals, medicines, cosmetics, and seduction. We send our prayers to the spirit world through the vapors of our burnt offerings. In East African cultures, the fragrance of smoldering incense (called *bakhoor* in Arabic) is said to feed the soul. Perfume (from the Latin for "through smoke") contains the essential oils of a plant, an extraction of the spirit of nature. Through the practice of aromatherapy, scent has been connected to stress reduction, physical and spiritual well-being, and even consumerism. Shoppers spend more in stores that smell like fresh linen.

As much as people have pleasant associations with floral, woodsy, and spicy scents, we also inhale toxins and pollutants. The Clean Air Act of 1970 was enacted by the US Congress to control the dangerous levels of air pollution, smog, acid rain, and ozone depletion harming the planet. We must remain vigilant and committed to environmental protection legislation and the reduction of all noxious emissions.

VI
pp quasi niente
quasi niente
pp quasi niente
SCENT

SCRYING CIRCLES

Scrying Circles were believed to be practiced by the Swamp Witches in the Louisiana Bayou as a form of divination and as a method to make predictions from a distance. A scrying circle is created by a medium who inscribes a circle in chalk on a wooden table. This enclosing circle metaphorically creates a facsimile of the physical location to be studied. The circle is then bisected by drawing the four cardinal directions. From the site itself, the medium collects a handful of earth, a few rocks, a leaf and twig, and a jar of water which are then placed in the quadrants according to their relative locations on the actual site. Subtle changes in the soil from moisture to dryness, for example, can indicate changes in weather. Over time, the leaves, flowers, herbs, and twigs are analyzed to detect any changes in smell or texture. The leaves will be observed for movement and the twigs for shaking or twitching. Any changes in the shadow patterns from the sticks or twigs are also followed closely. The water in the jar is read to gain insight to any water spirit activity. Finally, the rocks are then placed on top of one another to detect vibrations that can interpret any changes on the site.

As mentioned in the Water Jar card, scrying is an ancient practice in which an individual investigates a natural material to detect various messages or visions. When anyone—a landscape architect, architect, planner, engineer—studies a map, they are engaged in a form of divination and scrying. When a site plan or site design is created, it is in a sense making a prediction for the future.

VII
NORTH
WEST
EAST
SOUTH
SCRYING CIRCLES

PORTALS

A portal is an entryway to another dimension; on the other side is a new land. In our vocabulary the portal represents a shift in consciousness, the promise of an alternate reality. We cross a threshold to the land of enchantment in the space between sleeping and waking, between inside and out, at the edge of the forest, or where sea meets land. Envisioning portals, as a manifestation of the Air element, can raise our awareness of the landscape systems around us.

In ancient legend and in contemporary fiction, portals—symbolized by doorways, gates, caves, and crevices, as well as closets, bridges, telephone booths, and even train platform 9¾!—represent places of transformation and enlightenment. Today, the existence of black holes and wormholes in the spacetime continuum first hypothesized by Albert Einstein and Nathan Rosen are being tested by contemporary astrophysicists. Researchers at NASA are examining points in space where the earth's magnetic field comes in contact with the solar wind as possible sites of portals.

Portals are also part of the ecological web of life. Insects and animals enter and exit their habitats through portals. Snakes and lizards emerge from cracks in rock formations; they were understood by many Indigenous peoples as messengers from the underworld. Burrowing animals and desert species access the safety and cooler temperatures of their underground homes through the holes they dig in the earth. Observing their behavior can shed light on changing weather patterns. Bats search for portals and cavities in structures and tree trunks to make their roosts. They emerge as darkness falls, flying at the border between day and night, and bearing otherworldly traits of both bird and mammal.

VIII

PORTALS

WILL-O-WISP

For many centuries people have described seeing mysterious lights in forests, glens, and marshes at night. Accounts of these weird floating phosphorescent lights have been reported on every continent, with the first recorded vision in 1340 by Welsh poet Dafydd ap Gwilym.

What are these strange phenomena? They have been called many things: Fox Fire, Fairy Lights, Corpse Candles, Ghost Lights, Elf-Fire, and Jack-O-Lantern, to name a few. William Shakespeare mentions *ignis fatuus*, or "foolish fire," in his play *Henry IV*; Isaac Newton reported on *ignis fatuus* in his 18th-century text on optics. These elusive and ephemeral lights have been described as luminous, dancing flames, sometimes with bluish edges and yellow glowing interiors. They appear at night in isolated, low-lying landscapes such as swamps, bogs, or deep dark woodlands. On approach, they seem capable of moving away from the viewer, never letting anyone get too close.

Science has attempted to describe the will-o-wisp as a flame-like phosphorescence caused by gases from decaying plants in marshy areas, but there has been no conclusive explanation. Myths and superstitions surround them. In many folkloric traditions these lights are believed to be spirits of the dead, fairies, or a variety of other supernatural beings attempting to lead travelers off their course. They are also thought to be powerful omens able to predict the future. Perhaps the lesson here is to never abandon our belief in the magic of the landscape and to always be open to receiving the messages that nature is trying to communicate.

IX

WILL-O-WISP

HELIOTROPISM

Heliotropism is the term used to describe the movement of plants in response to the position of the sun. The sunflower (*Helianthus annuus*) is a common example. Young sunflowers anticipate the sunrise each morning and turn their heads east to maximize their exposure to the sun's energy. This process provides optimal conditions for photosynthesis, pollination, fertilization, and seed development.

Heliotropism is an example of a circadian rhythm. Plants, animals, and people all respond to their environments with an internal timekeeping process based on a roughly-twenty-four-hour cycle of day and night caused by the earth's rotation on its axis. The ability of plants to measure time, to respond to the daily and seasonal changes in their environments, helps them thrive. Their internal clocks regulate when they should expend energy to open their flowers and release their fragrance, as well as when they should conserve energy to survive.

Sunflowers are native to North America and Mesoamerica and were first domesticated thousands of years ago. They are an important food source, and a key ingredient in medicines and dyes of Indigenous peoples. The sunflower symbolizes an abundant harvest to the Hopi, and is also part of Iroquois cosmology. In Greek mythology, the oceanid Clytie transformed into a sunflower so she could trace the movement of Apollo, the god of the sun, on his daily journey; thus the sunflower also represents loyalty and constancy. The image of a sunflower has been used in recent history to represent nuclear disarmament, and is a contemporary symbol of the Ukrainian resistance movement.

X

HELIOTROPISM

POLLINATORS

Pollinator decline is one form of global change that has the potential to alter the shape and structure of the world. It is a bad omen when an ecosystem loses its large mammals, but an even worse sign is when it can no longer support its insects. It is frightening to think that our commercial beekeepers are reporting up to 45.5% losses of their hive populations. We can no longer count on wild pollinators to make up this difference because we've so altered the landscape that many are no longer viable. The loss of our pollinators is an incredibly alarming trend; we must continue to provide appropriate food sources and habitats for them, and respect their role as spiritual messengers.

One of the many wonders of nature is the bee dance in which bees communicate to the hive the distance and location of nectar sources through elaborate flight patterns and tail wagging. Bees can also see colors that humans cannot, and are attracted to the ultraviolet patterns on flowers. In Egyptian mythology bees were believed to be the tears of the sun god Ra. In ancient Greece, Artemis, goddess of nature, oversaw the territories of wild bees. The Mayan god Ah Muzen was also a god of bees and their honey. Bees and their magical nectar were sacred to the Irish goddess Brigid.

Butterflies, moths, and hummingbirds are also excellent pollinators. Psyche, the Greek goddess of the soul, is often represented with butterfly wings. In Aztec religion, the warrior goddess Ītzpāpālōt was known as the "Obsidian Butterfly." Huitzilopochtli, the god of sun and war, and one of the most important deities in the Aztec pantheon, was often represented as a hummingbird. In the Philippines, Ibu was the goddess of moths and creation.

XI
POLLINATORS

OUROBOROS

The image of a snake curled in a circle and appearing to eat its own tail is a symbol found throughout time and across cultures. Known in the West as an *ouroboros*, the nearly universal motif can be seen on neolithic Chinese pottery, dynastic Egyptian funerary objects, ancient Greek manuscripts, Renaissance alchemical texts, and myriad artifacts from around the world. In Icelandic tradition, Hindu religion, Huichol culture, and many other mythologies, the ouroboros is a cosmological emblem, symbolizing the creation of the world. As a spherical symbol the coiled snake represents many different ideas, including those of boundary, order, continuity, the union of opposites, renewal, interconnection, and eternity. Twisted on itself, the ouroboros forms a figure eight—a sign of infinity.

The knowledge of balance implied by the ouroboros can be extended to ecological thought. In a broad context, ecology represents a unity of self and world, of the physical and the spiritual. An ecosystem is a self-contained and renewable unit, ordered by the cycles of nature. Interestingly, the shift in cycles became evident during the coronavirus pandemic when human interactions and activities were reduced and nature rebounded. Birdsong was more cacophonous than freeway noise.

The concept of regenerative systems as represented by an ouroboros was a key component in the development of environmental design theory and practice in the 1970s, particularly in the field of passive architectural design. Passive design relies on natural methods of heating and cooling rather than on energy-intensive and non-renewable resources. As pioneers of what today is called the sustainability movement in the United States, designers explored the interdependence of built structure and landscape to create functional microclimates. This wisdom exists in many parts of the world as traditional ecological knowledge.

XII
OUROBOROS

THE STAG

Coming upon a deer in the woods is always an unexpected magical moment; this creature of the forest mystically appears and then lopes away. The stag was one of the first universal mythological gods to be worshiped as a protector and keeper of the forest secrets. This can be surmised by the numerous cave paintings and petroglyphs representing the stag as a supernatural being. It follows that prehistoric cave paintings and petroglyphs from around the world portray male and female shamans with the horns of a stag. The grave of the Bad Dürrenberg shaman is the oldest burial in central Germany and contains the body of a female buried 9,000 years ago with an elaborate headdress of deer antlers.

Many global myths involve the stag. One of the earliest stag gods emerged in Mesopotamia as the Sumerian Dara-Mah or Great Stag. In Celtic mythology the stag was the symbol of the god of the forest and wild animals known as Cernunnos, or "The Horned One." Historically portrayed with antlers, this pagan god was absorbed into the canon of Christian doctrine as the Vision of Saint Eustace. The story goes that the Roman general Placidus was out hunting a stag when an image of Jesus on the cross appeared to him between the animal's antlers. So moved by the apparition, Placidus converted to Christianity and adopted the name Eustace.

The spirit of the forest is kept alive in contemporary culture as fictional entities in popular science fantasy novels and movies. In Hayao Miyazaki's film *Princess Mononoke*, the deer god is the mystical keeper of the forest, a wonderous creature with antler-like branches. Look for him next time you are in the woods.

XIII
THE STAG

DRAGON VEIN

From the Gates of Babylon to the *Game of Thrones* dragons are humankind's familiar; they exist as images on artifacts and as totems of our collective imaginations whose likeness has endured since antiquity. A dragon is a composite figure, part reptile, part mammal, part bird of any color. Some dragons dwell in clouds while others make their homes in caves; some are depicted as fire-breathing beasts and others as more gentle giants. Dragons appear in myths and legends worldwide as guardians and allies as well as ogres and assassins; they protect as well as destroy. In Western traditions dragons are typically portrayed as evil, winged demons associated with greed and corruption; in Eastern traditions dragons appear more sinuous and magnificent, their power associated with wisdom, strength, and support. A dragon embodies potential energy.

In Chinese folklore, dragon veins are lines of energy, or *qi*, that flow across mountain peaks. Mountains are sacred landforms in many cultures, as places where heaven and earth meet. The dragon vein originates in the clouds and undulates across the range, tracing the spine of a dragon. The vein continues downslope in meandering stream channels. In an ecological sense, the dragon vein outlines a watershed, and can be thought of as a tool of landscape analysis; it is used by geomancers to determine an ideal site for habitation. Auspicious sites are embraced by mountains, often forming a U-shape, and crossed by a flowing river. Assessment is informed by a deep understanding of the concentrated energy and interrelationship of mountain and river systems—a manifestation of the power of the dragon.

XIV
DRAGON VEIN

WOOD

In this suit we draw from Eastern traditions to incorporate the elemental energy of wood as a manifestation of the spirit of the natural world. The Taoist philosophy of the five elements expresses the dynamic balance of the universe through the interactions of earth, metal, fire, water, and wood. Fire can destroy wood, yet wood can feed fire; wood can break earth, yet earth can bury wood. The attributes of each element derive not only from its physical characteristics but also its metaphysical properties; achieving harmony through consciousness is the goal. Wood is associated with the capacity for creative growth and emergence, as represented by the spring season.

We interpret wood broadly as representative of the entire plant kingdom and examine the symbolism of plants and their roles in various cultural practices that are based on an awareness of their ecological value. An ecosystem is a complex network reliant on keystone plant species. Without plants there would be no life on earth. Plants provide food, habitat, medicine, even the air we breathe. Less obvious are the functions that plants perform in controlling erosion, preventing floods and landslides, pollinating crops, and storing carbon.

KOKOPELLI

Kokopelli is commonly recognized as the Hopi curved-back fluteplayer whose image first appeared on petroglyphs and Hohokam pottery over a thousand years ago. To many Indigenous groups in the American Southwest his spirit is associated with fertility of the land and the people. He is the harbinger of spring, a conveyor of resources, and transmitter of knowledge. There are many different interpretations of Kokopelli's likeness and significance; he has been portrayed as a wandering storyteller, trickster, rainmaker, musician, seducer, and buffoon, whose flute playing spreads magic and mayhem as well as abundance and favorable auspices across the land.

To Puebloan peoples, Kokopelli is the ancestral spirit of the contemporaneous Flute Player Clan. His image incised on rocks and stones is believed to mark the historical migration patterns of their kin. Kokopelli is also the Hopi term given to a pair of male and female *kachinas* (or divine spirit beings) whose embodiment through dance and figurative art is used to communicate traditional social values.

Kokopelli is often described as "hump-backed," an imperfect form, or a figure weighted down by the burden he carries. His image may have been inspired by the shape of an insect, such as an ant. In some versions of his story the sack he carries may be filled with seeds, a metaphor for the cultivation of wisdom and growth.

I

KOKOPELLI

KODAMA

When you walk through the deep forest, do you ever have the feeling that something is lurking beyond, watching you? You are, in fact, being watched by thousands of pairs of eyes, from the creatures, insects, and even microorganisms who know you are there and are carefully monitoring your movements. You are in their domain.

One explanation for this phenomenon originates with the *kodama*—the woodland spirits in ancient and contemporary Japanese folklore. The word is also used to describe the tree in which the spirits might be living. Difficult to see, the kodama are very nimble and scurry around remote woodlands. They are said to have the mysterious power of invisibility, being able to appear and disappear at will.

In Hayao Miyazaki's film, *Princess Mononoke,* the Kodama are envisioned as spirits of the forest, represented as small, playful figures dwelling in tree canopies and the forest floor. They help create a feeling of mystery, observing people who step into the forest. The forest, in Miyazaki's rendering, is not just a collection of vegetation but a site with deep spiritual meaning. In his film, the kodama are portrayed as small, white creatures with large, rattling heads and mask-like faces, inhabiting ancient and beautiful trees.

Some of us can see the kodama and others cannot. They are always present, but don't always make their presence known. They are neutral observers, beyond good and evil. How can we work in concert with our fellow creatures on this planet and forge a symbiotic relationship? Miyazaki feels that the solution to our environmental problems is to discard our old ways of thinking and work in accord with the spirits of place.

II

KODAMA

KUPALA

Kupala is the Slavic goddess of midsummer. She is associated with the celebrations and rituals of the summer solstice, the longest day of the year, when the sun is at its highest and most powerful position. Fire, water, and plants figure in Kupala folklore. Acts of burning and submerging have the effects of healing and regeneration, and of cleansing. The color and fragrance of flowers are at their seasonal peaks and are symbolic of joy and desire.

In traditional Eastern European cultural practices, bonfires were lit from hay and other materials contributed by all people in the community to honor the sun. To not do so was believed to bring misfortune. The higher up a slope that a fire was lit, the closer its affinity to the sun. Straw wheels and straw maidens were also fabricated and set ablaze. Jumping over these flaming objects was symbolic of a rite of restoration, a purification of sorts.

As part of the traditional festival of Kupala, young women would weave wreaths from herbs and flowers they gathered at dawn on the solstice, and then float them in a body of water, illuminated by candles. Whomever "hooked" the wreath was destined to partner with the wreath maker. Ferns were also significant to Kupala as an instrument of humility. Legend has it that on Kupala Night, when the spirits of nature were most active, a magical fern would flower in the forest and bring wealth and eternal youth to the finder. Those who sought the flowering fern would protect themselves with mugwort to repel the malevolent forces. However, the fortune came at a cost; it could not be shared.

IIII

KUPALA

THE MAYPOLE

The beginning of May sets off a flurry of events in which the Rites of Spring are celebrated throughout the entire month. Almost every calendar day marks a pagan observance of the rebirth of nature and a rejoicing of the return of Summer and its warmth. The Maypole tradition is one of the most well-known of these ancient spring traditions and has survived into the 21st century. The first recorded Maypole celebration dates from the 14th century in central Wales. It is thought to have originated as a fertility rite in Scotland, Wales, and Germany, where the participants sang and danced around a living tree. The living tree evolved into a tall wooden pole, wrapped in brightly colored ribbons and capped with decorative garlands of flowers.

The ritual is performed by pairs of boys and girls or men and women who begin by standing in alternating pairs around the base of the pole, each holding the end of a different colored ribbon. Symbolic of the ancient mating and fertility rite, they then begin to dance, weaving around each other, with males and females going in different directions and intertwining with one another until they are joined as couples at the base of the maypole. Many people came to consider the celebration a scandalous, lewd, and lascivious public display of sexual coupling, and the dance was outlawed in many parts of Europe during the Protestant Reformation.

Today, the Rites of Spring endure in a variety of ways, including spring cleaning and clearing activities, meditation, eating certain foods likes eggs, and bringing flowers and color into the home. Around the globe, the communal celebration of the creation of new life remains an important event.

IV

THE MAYPOLE

SEED BANKS

A seed is a promise for the future, a storehouse of potential. Seeds produce plants from which all life depends; they are invaluable treasures, sources of food and productive landscapes such as grasslands, prairies, and woodlands. Many creation myths begin with the story of a seed. Throughout history seeds have been regarded as currency and traded across the globe. Plants evolved and adapted naturally to these varied geographies, inheriting survival traits from their parents. Hybrid species are bred to be exact copies; their seeds are sterile and will not regenerate.

A seed bank is a storage facility that preserves genetic diversity. Deposits and withdrawals are made for conservation and restoration purposes. As the world's climates are changing and species become extinct, a seed bank will ensure a biodiverse future. However, not all seeds can be stored, including about one-third of currently endangered species. The Svalbard Global Seed Vault in Norway stores over a million varieties of seeds from food crops around the world. The Millennium Seed Bank in England contains more than 2 billion seeds, and aims to preserve 25% of the world's plants or about 75,000 different species.

Seeds are also repositories of the past, containers of cultural histories and memories, particularly in the context of food and edible plants. Keeping ancestral traditions alive, people collect and exchange heirloom seeds. Today, farmers of color in America are cultivating fruits and vegetables of the African and Afro-Caribbean diaspora in an effort to promote food sovereignty in the Black community and equity in the agricultural industry. In Africa, seed activists are fighting corporate agricultural interests to maintain their right to plant indigenous, non-hybridized seeds.

V

SEED BANKS

AGAVE SPIRIT

Have you ever wondered why alcohol is called spirits? Alcohol is made using the alchemical process of distillation in which the essence, or spirit, of a plant is transformed into alcohol. As almost every alcoholic drink comes from a plant, it is no exception that Mezcal is extracted from the agave plant and has its origins in Aztec mythology.

Mayahuel is the Aztec Goddess associated with the agave plant and the liquor made from it. This female deity was one of the several goddesses who protected and supported fertility. According to ancient Oaxacan myth, Mayahuel fell in love with a human, became pregnant, and at the end of a brutal winter gave birth to 400 rabbits, an allegory for the numerous stages of inebriation. According to lore, one of the rabbits set off on a journey to obtain fire and, once finding it, jumped in and became an Alebrije fire spirit. This fire spirt then jumped into the heart of the agave plant creating Mezcal, a "holy elixir," known as the goddess's gift to the Aztec gods.

As an expression of gratitude, Mayahuel covered the hills of Oaxaca with a wide variety of agave species. All 160 different species of Agave come from the Oaxaca region of Mexico, one of the most biodiverse ecosystems in Mexico. The Mezcal made from each variety of agave plant has its own unique medical and spiritual qualities. The ingestion of this sacred elixir is considered a sacrament, and is not only a spirit but also a gift from the gods.

VI
AGAVE SPIRIT

SACRED LOTUS

To be like the lotus is to be of the earth and of the air, to be grounded yet unbound. To sit in the lotus position is to have your lower body in contact with the earth and your torso extended toward the heavens, a balance of weight, energy, and spirit. The form and growth pattern of the aquatic perennial plant *Nelumbo nucifera*, or Sacred Lotus, is by nature aspirational. Native to southeast Asia, the lotus takes root in the murky bottoms of lakes and ponds and shoots up stems (rhizomes) through the water to produce beautiful flowers that rise above the surface. The flower petals close at night and the blossom sinks below the water only to reappear with the light of the next day. These characteristics make the lotus a symbol of resilience, rebirth, enlightenment, purity, and transcendence. The sacred lotus has spiritual significance in Buddhist and Hindu religions. Buddha is often depicted seated on a lotus flower, as are Vishnu and Lakshmi. In the ancient Egyptian cult of the dead, the lotus symbolizes resurrection. In Japan the lotus blooming season is observed with viewing festivals and harvest celebrations.

The lotus plant is remarkable in many ways. Its seeds remain viable and can germinate after thousands of years. The stems, flowers, and seeds of the sacred lotus are important sources of food, as well as key ingredients in ayurvedic and Chinese medicines. In addition to its culinary and medicinal uses *Nelumbo nucifera* is also a phytoremediator, capable of removing toxins from contaminated surface water. The sacred lotus is a phenomenal gift and emblem of regeneration.

VII

SACRED LOTUS

BOTTLE TREES

The ability to produce hollow glass bottles was developed around 1600 BCE in Mesopotamia and Egypt. Hollow glass bottles eventually made their way down to the Congo region of Africa in the 9th century. It was during this era that the tradition of bottle trees took root. Empty bottles produce eerie sounds when wind passes over the mouth of the bottle, frightening and chasing away malevolent spirits. Since blue is a color especially reviled by evil spirits, blue glass bottles were considered ideal. It was also thought that the color blue had a healing aura.

The blue bottles were suspended upside down on trees to ward off evil. Bottle trees, as they became called, were strategically placed near important public gathering spaces and at intersections to defend against passing wicked spirits. This indigenous tradition of bottle tree magic was carried to Trinidad, the Bahamas, Haiti, and the American south through the Atlantic slave trade in the 17th century. Enslaved African people not only placed bottles on trees but also lined pathways to protect their homes and gardens. It was believed that during the night the spirits were attracted to the bottles by their bright colors, and once inside were destroyed by the morning sunlight.

There are interesting similarities between the traditional Haitian Mabou Tree of Souls and the Tree of Souls in James Cameron's film *Avatar*. The Tree of Souls is the mother tree of the fictional Navi people, and is of extreme spiritual significance in their religion.

VIII

BOTTLE TREES

LULAV AND ETROG

The Jewish Festival of the Tabernacles, called *Sukkot*, is a celebration of thanksgiving for the bounty of the earth and its capacity to shelter and sustain community during pilgrimage. The fall holiday is rooted in agricultural tradition; people express gratitude for the harvest and pray for rain to nourish the land next season.

During the holiday, it is customary to gather cuttings and specimens from plants that represent the four ecosystems or landscape types of Israel—the desert, mountains, rivers, and agricultural lowlands. A closed palm frond, three myrtle boughs, and two willow branches are bound together into a *lulav* and waved during religious services, along with a citron fruit, or *etrog*. Together, the *lulav* and *etrog* represent "the four species" and are offered to the six directions—forward, back, left, right, up, down—acknowledging the divine forces that surround us, and asking for blessings.

The meanings of the Hebrew words for the four species are associated with the shapes and characteristics of the plants; tied together they represent unity and balance. They are also symbolic of the fertility of the land and the patterns of rainfall. The date palm is a tall, upright tree with abundant fruit, it can sway in the wind and not break. Common myrtle is a Mediterranean plant with aromatic leaves and showy white flowers. Myrtle is associated with the Greek goddesses Demeter and Aphrodite, and the Roman goddess Venus, who emerged from the sea holding a sprig of myrtle. Willows are water-loving plants with flexible branches and strong roots; they are used to control erosion and restore habitats. Citron, like lemon, is a fragrant fruit used in the cuisine and traditional medicines of many cultures.

IX

LULAV AND ETROG

THE THREE FRIENDS OF WINTER

Chinese garden design is strongly intertwined with symbolism and magic. Any unusual changes in the plants could foretell good or bad fortune. For elder Chinese philosophers, trees and flowers were not only garden elements, but also illustrative of human feeling and aspirations. Plants in the garden were imbued with metaphorical meaning. The Three Friends of Winter describe the characteristics of pine, bamboo, and plum—pine is evergreen and upright, symbolizing virtue and longevity; bamboo sways with the wind, symbolizing resilience; and plum blossoms emerge radiant on bare branches, symbolizing endurance. All are mentioned in a 9th-century poem by Zhu Qingyu.

In the garden, pine trees were prized for their contorted sculptural shapes and their ability to remain green throughout the year; the bamboo for its flickering shadows, graceful swaying, and the hypnotic sound of the wind sweeping thought its leaves; and the plum was planted not only for its beautiful branching tracery but also for the delightful effect its bountiful cloud-blossoms had on admirers.

In China, landscape painting and garden design are almost inseparable. In landscape painting, a fascinating relationship exists between painting and magic. It was believed that great painters were also great magicians, and there was no line between the painter and the supernatural. The more talented the painter the stronger the spell woven into the painting.

X

THE THREE FRIENDS OF WINTER

MANDRAKE

Few other plants in the world are as notorious as the mandrake. The distinctive shape of this perennial herb, with its forked taproot resembling human limbs, has provoked people's imaginations for thousands of years, endowing the plant with magical and medicinal powers. Native to Mediterranean regions and a member of the Solanaceae or "deadly nightshade" family, the plant contains narcotic alkaloids and is highly poisonous. Mentioned in ancient cuneiform, Arabic, and Greek texts, mandrake has been used throughout history as an anesthetic, aphrodisiac, curative, talisman, and hex.

Botanists in medieval Europe believed in the "doctrine of signatures," wherein a plant's appearance was related to its healing properties. Mandrake roots can look like human infants and thus were thought to enhance fertility; women wanting to bear a child would sleep with a mandrake beneath their pillow. The Greek pharmacologist Dioscorides believed there were male and female mandrakes.

There are many myths and beliefs relating to the anthropomorphic characteristics of the mandrake. As a stemless herb with a large root, mandrake is connected to ideas of the underworld. Legend has it that when pulled from the earth the plant emits a scream that is fatal to all who hear it. The root was also thought to emit light and vapors. Part human and part devil, the root was both a good luck charm and a tool of sorcery. A mandrake root dressed in doll's clothing would help one find buried treasure. Women carrying mandrake roots were burned for practicing witchcraft. The Greek goddess Circe used mandrake to turn men into pigs. Mandrake is featured in popular works of contemporary fiction and film, including the *Harry Potter* series and *Pan's Labyrinth*.

XI
MANDRAKE

THE FLOWERY MEAD

The Flowery Mead, or wildflower meadow, might have evolved from the Homeric myth of the Elysian Fields—the beautiful rolling meadows full of flowers and grasses where the righteous would spend their afterlife. Like a miniature Elysian field, the Flowery Mead is one of the primary elements of the medieval garden in western Europe, usually the centerpiece of a small, enclosed space. To produce the effect of a bejeweled lawn, the grass was often pounded flat with a large wooden hammer, creating a smooth green canvas to highlight the flowers. The meadow was typically composed of primroses, marigolds, violets, columbines, lilies, irises, cornflowers, carnations, and roses. The effect was one not of order but of a semi-wild grassy meadow. This open lawn provided a pleasant, uninterrupted view of a field sparkling with dots of flowers.

The Unicorn Tapestries, woven between 1495-1505 and on display at The Cloisters, a property of the Metropolitan Museum of Art in New York, provide excellent renditions of what a flowery mead might have looked like. The *millefleur* or "thousand flowers" style was a common background for French tapestry in the 15th century. There are over one hundred depictions of flowers in these tapestries of which eighty have been botanically identified.

The flowery mead is an idealization of an ordered nature where one can find repose after a leading a good life. As a metaphor, it is not unlike the depiction of heaven as a flower-filled garden. But danger may lurk within the beauty; we must remain aware of the ramifications of our actions. When Persephone collected the enchanting narcissus from a flowery mead, the earth opened up and she was abducted into the underworld.

XII
THE FLOWERY MEAD

ARCADIA

Arcadia is a term used to describe an idyllic landscape where people coexist with rustic nature shielded from the corruption of urban society, a utopian ideal of peace and harmony reminiscent of the Golden Age of antiquity. Since ancient times Arcadia has been represented in poems and paintings as a rural paradise of lush forests, mountain sanctuaries, green pastures, and flowing streams, unspoiled by humans, and populated by nymphs, satyrs, and other deities. In Greek mythology, Arcadia is the home of Pan, god of the wilderness; the Roman poet Virgil set his *Eclogues* in Arcadia.

"Et in Arcadia, Ego" is the phrase etched on a stone monument depicted in the 17th-century painting, *Arcadian Shepherds*, by Nicolas Poussin. Uncovered by the shepherds as they tend to their flock, there are various interpretations of the meaning of this famous promise: *In Arcadia, I am.* Over the centuries, the phrase has inspired many works of art and literature reflecting on the theme of pastoral simplicity and virtue, and the idea of reclaiming lost innocence—nostalgia for a time and place when humans lived in concert with nature.

Throughout history peoples' attitudes toward nature have shifted from positions of dominance and control to perspectives of mutual dependence and stewardship. "Arcadian ecology" refers to an ethics of coexistence with nature rather than human supremacy. In this framework, nature is not an "other," an external resource to be exploited, but rather a life force to be respected and valued equally. Arcadia embodies the spirit of kinship and unity.

XIII

ARCADIA

THE SACRED GROVE

Pagans believe that the forest is our primal birthplace and the original habitation of our ancestors. Historically, sacred groves were dedicated to the fertility cults of Artemis and Apollo by the Greeks. Later, the Romans consecrated Arcadia as the domain of Pan, the god of unrestrained natural forces. Our original religious structures evolved out of the sacred grove, where the trunks of trees evoke building columns and the vegetative canopy resembles a roof. Evidence of a sacred grove, as described by the 2nd-century CE Greek travel writer Pausanias, has been confirmed by archaeologists at the ancient site of Nemea in the Peloponnese peninsula. The Temple of Zeus was sited within a large forest of stately cypress trees planted closely together to create mysterious effects with its dappled shadows and shifting light.

Sacred groves lie at the core of many religious traditions and at one time in our ancient history were most likely found on every continent in the world. Unfortunately, most have vanished. Osun-Osogbo, in Nigeria, is one of the last remaining sacred groves. Several centuries old, it is located along the banks of the Osun River adjacent to the city of Osogbo. In Yoruba belief system, the river is represented by the goddess Osun, protector of her people in the region. Historically, there were numerous sacred groves lining the river, but most have been destroyed by urbanization.

XIV

THE SACRED GROVE

EARTH

Earth is the most fundamental of the elements that constitute the world. Plato represented earth as a cube, the most stable form and the primary geometrical solid from which were generated the other more ephemeral elements of Fire, Air, and Water. Earth is our foundation, the source that sustains our bodies and souls. Life is rooted in earth; it is a medium for growth. We cultivate earth to be nourished; we build with earth to be sheltered; we bury in earth to preserve and return home. We sometimes think of earth as land, and use many words that derive from the Latin, *terra*, to describe various aspects and features of earth. We are literally and figuratively grounded on the planet Earth, yet land covers less than 30% of the Earth's surface.

In this final suit, we examine a variety of ways in which humans have understood and respected the earth as our physical and spiritual home. Natural topographic features, like caves and mountains, are a part of many cultures' creation myths. Human-made forms, like mounds, mazes, berms, and bridges, are part of place-making strategies, ways for people to center themselves and propitiate the forces of nature. Earth has protected us since the time of our first breath; we must be mindful to return the favor.

CAVES

Humans emerged out of the earth. Caves were our first shelters and our first religious sanctuaries. During the Ice Age caves served not only as human residences but also as arenas for the development of religious art. The Occitanie region of France is the epicenter of cave paintings and the location of the Pech Merle Cave. Pech Merle is thirty-five miles east of Cahor, the location of some of the most amazing cave paintings in history. The caves are filled with dramatic paintings of spotted horses, mammoths, bisons, aurochs, and bears painted as early as 2500 BCE with later work dated to the 17th century BCE. The site also contains a stunning handprint of what is believed to be one of the first signatures by a female artist.

The cave evolved to become a central symbolic element of the Zoroastrian religion, which is considered one of the first organized religions from three and a half thousand years ago. The Charsteen cave, located near Duhok, Iraq, is the oldest Zoroastrian shrine dating from the first millennium BCE.

The cave was an important element in the performance of the Eleusinian Mysteries, an initiation rite for the cult of Demeter and Persephone in ancient Greece. The cave of Persephone at Eleusis was the site of the annual celebration of the rebirth of spring, reenacted as the mystery of Persephone's return from the underworld. Participants would first enter Pluto's cave during a full moon. On their journey they would descend from the light into the darkness where they endured fear, loss of hope, and the sense of death. The experience of re-emerging into the light of the Elysian park on the other side was symbolic of a transformative rebirth.

I
CAVES

ECHOES

Have you ever spoken to the mountains, and received an answer in return? In Greek mythology, Echo is the name of an Oread, or mountain nymph, who was cursed by the goddess Hera to only repeat the words of others. An echo is a phenomenon of sound reflecting off a distant surface. The farther away the object, the more time it takes for the sound to return.

Many nocturnal and marine animals are sensitive to sound, and navigate, hunt, and forage by echolocation. Bats, dolphins, and whales emit sounds in a variety of ways and use echoes to identify the shape and location of different elements and creatures in the darkness of night and depths of the oceans. Sound travels faster through water than air, which makes "biological" sonar an efficient process.

Sonar, radar, and lidar are all contemporary technologies that use echoes to map things on earth that we can't see, in essence giving a voice to the landscape. Sonar (Sound Navigation and Ranging) measures echoes from sound waves and is used to map the ocean floor. "Active" sonar has been known to cause acoustic trauma to whales, prompting legislation to curtail its use in certain regions. Radar uses radio waves to measure the size, quantity, speed, and direction of moving objects. Meteorologists predict weather patterns based on radar data from the interior of clouds. Lidar measures light reflected from laser pulses to accurately map the three-dimensional structure of the earth's surface. Lidar can sense topographic features below a forest canopy and is an effective tool for environmental planning and landscape management.

Since time immemorial we call out to the land and listen for its wise response.

II

1300 GCT 28.XI.58 10/4 #1074
00°15' S 39°42' W
Temp. 27.3
1500 GCT
00°14.5' S
Temp. 27.5
2000 GCT 28.XI.58 11/4
00°18.2' S 40°38.2' W
Temp. 27.4
METERS
BT 18460-8 5-8-58

ECHOES

THE PRIMROSE PATH

There is hardly a culture in the world that does not have some form of traditional belief in little people. They may take different forms or have different names, but all appear to have similar traits. Nowhere is the Faerie Faith more prevalent than in the Celtic countries of Ireland, Scotland, Wales, England, and Brittany, and with it is a specific relationship of the faerie folk to flowers. For instance, Bluebells are especially revered by faeries, but they are also very dangerous to humans. If you wander into a ring of Bluebells, you might fall under the spell of a faerie enchantment. Also, you must be wary of ever disturbing the Bluebells, for if perchance you brush one of its flowers it can disrupt the spells which faeries place on the petals.

The Primrose Path has its origins in Celtic faerie mythology, and the flower has many legends associated with it. It boasts the unique power of making the invisible visible—eating primroses would allow you to see the faerie folk! On May Day, bouquets of primroses are hung over doors and windows to repel black magic and misfortune, only allowing white magic to enter. Being led down the Primrose Path means that one has been diverted from the straight and narrow pathway of purpose and taken an unexpected detour. Traveling down the Primrose Path means we are now open to enchantment, enlightenment, and magic. The direct route is what is expected but is not always the most rewarding.

Follow the trail of these lovely flowers and you will be rewarded with the unexpected. This is the path of life changing and mind-altering revelation.

III

THE PRIMROSE PATH

THE LABYRINTH

Walking a labyrinth is an ancient form of communication with the earth. Eyes focused down, our bodies follow a narrow path, circling and meandering along a single line of movement choreographed to never cross itself. We move to and from the center of the form—the midway point of our journey—only to retrace our steps and end up where we began, for truly, the journey is the destination. The labyrinth represents a metaphorical pilgrimage.

Spatially, one can't get lost in a labyrinth—the mind may wander, but the body can take no wrong turns. Unlike a maze, which has multiple paths, a labyrinth is an intricately wound, one-way path. There are no short cuts. Through recursive and repetitive movements, the labyrinth becomes a meditation, much like a mandala; time and direction are transcended.

Labyrinths or labyrinthine symbols appear on Celtic petroglyphs, Egyptian tombs, Greek coins, Roman mosaics, Tantric texts, Chinese palaces, medieval European cathedrals, and New Age gardens. They can be made of turf, stone, dirt, or gravel. In some cultures, the labyrinth is considered a protective sign. Neolithic or "classical" labyrinth patterns look more brain-like than later or "medieval" patterns which are clearly divided into quadrants with odd numbers of circuits or rings. Ancient labyrinths outlined by small stones can be found near the shores of Nordic countries and are believed to bring luck to fishermen. One of the most famous labyrinths is inscribed in the floor of the 13th century cathedral in Chartres, France, where Christians walk as a form of devotion and prayer.

A labyrinth is magical; we travel a great distance yet go nowhere.

IV

THE LABYRINTH

FAERIE HILLS

The mysterious Faerie Hills are located in a narrow glen near the northern coastal town of Uig, on the Isle of Skye, Scotland. When you approach this dramatic hidden landscape its looks as though you've stepped into a magical realm. Suddenly, a dramatic variety of conical hills, glens, and pools shift in and out of view. Its magical association could have come from local lore in which the faerie folk are said to live near pools of water and inhabit grassy knolls. It is easy to believe that mythical creatures created this otherworldly landscape.

When walking through the faerie hills of Skye you discover hills within hills, circles within circles; you lose your sense of direction when plunged into the ancient grove of gnarled, moss-draped dwarf oaks. The whimsical conical hills defy perspective. Some loom large and some shift underfoot as your sense of scale distorts. Eyes peer out at you from the grassy hills and faces take form on the rocks as you begin to sense strange and enchanted presences. As you climb up to the top of the hills and look down from this elevated viewpoint, your path looks entirely different, nothing through which you remember passing. When you descend, you enter yet another realm where your perceptions of reality are constantly being tested as your mind fights to explain these strange apparitions. If you try to count the number of conical hills, the count will always change. Some believe that there is a conical hill for each month of the year, but no one can keep count.

Here the mystical experience becomes attainable and somehow visitors from all over the world are driven to conduct their own private rituals, making labyrinths, stone circles, and devotional offerings.

V
FAERIE HILLS

FUNGI WEBS

The Earth has an Information Technology system as powerful and complex as any Silicon Valley startup. It is responsible for supporting the "wood-wide web" of plant communication and resource exchange, and goes by the name of *mycorrhiza*, or fungus root; mushroom, if you will. Mushrooms are the fruit (the only part we typically see) of the microscopic thread-like fungus called *mycelium*. Mycelium webs attach to the roots of trees and plants and are an important part of soil structure. This fungus-root relationship is called the mycorrhizal network.

Water, nutrients, and carbon are transferred through this network, and, as scientists are discovering, information can also be transmitted. The mycorrhizae function as a delivery system, forwarding messages in the form of enzymes to and from plants within the community, like nature's own Nextdoor app! Diseased trees or trees under attack will send out signals to neighboring trees warning them to build up their defenses; older trees will send carbon to support young seedlings.

Soil fungi are also proving to have powerful commercial and ecological value. Bricks manufactured from mycelium are a sustainable building material; through a process called mycoremediation, mycorrhizae absorb toxins from the soil and can decompose plastics.

Underground and microscopic, the fungi web operates 24/7 to keep the earth's ecosystems functioning. The network may be invisible to humans, but the mystical and healing properties of the mighty mushroom popping up through the soil have been well known throughout time and place. The mystery and magic of the mushroom prevails.

VI

FUNGI WEBS

HENGES

A henge is a prehistoric, banked, circular or oval earthen enclosure, dating from around 3000 BCE to 2000 BCE, during the Neolithic and early Bronze Ages. They are mostly found in Scotland and England. The Thornborough Henges are an unusual ritual landscape that includes three aligned henges extending for over a mile. Often referred to as the Stonehenge of the North, the complex is thought to have been part of a Neolithic and Bronze Age religious complex like those on the Salisbury Plain. The complex includes many large ancient structures including a cursus, burial grounds, and remnants of habitation. Archaeologists revealed that this complex was built on top of an existing cursus, which is a long narrow earthwork resembling the shape of a cigar. The southern section of the central circle is bisected by a cursus, which runs for approximately one mile.

The three henges are almost identical in size and composition, each having a diameter of approximately 780 feet and two large entrances situated directly opposite each other. The earth embankments were most likely covered with white chalk giving them a dazzling ephemeral appearance. The henges are located around 1,800 feet apart on an approximate northwest-southeast alignment. With the surveying abilities of these ancient engineers, it is strange how the southern alignment and circle bends slightly to the west. The three circular henges may have an astrological association with the three stars in Orion's belt.

Realizing that these three henges have traveled around the Sun more than 5,000 times only accentuates the mystery of our place in the universe. Even though we don't know who made these landscapes or what their purpose was, they still evoke powerful emotions.

VII

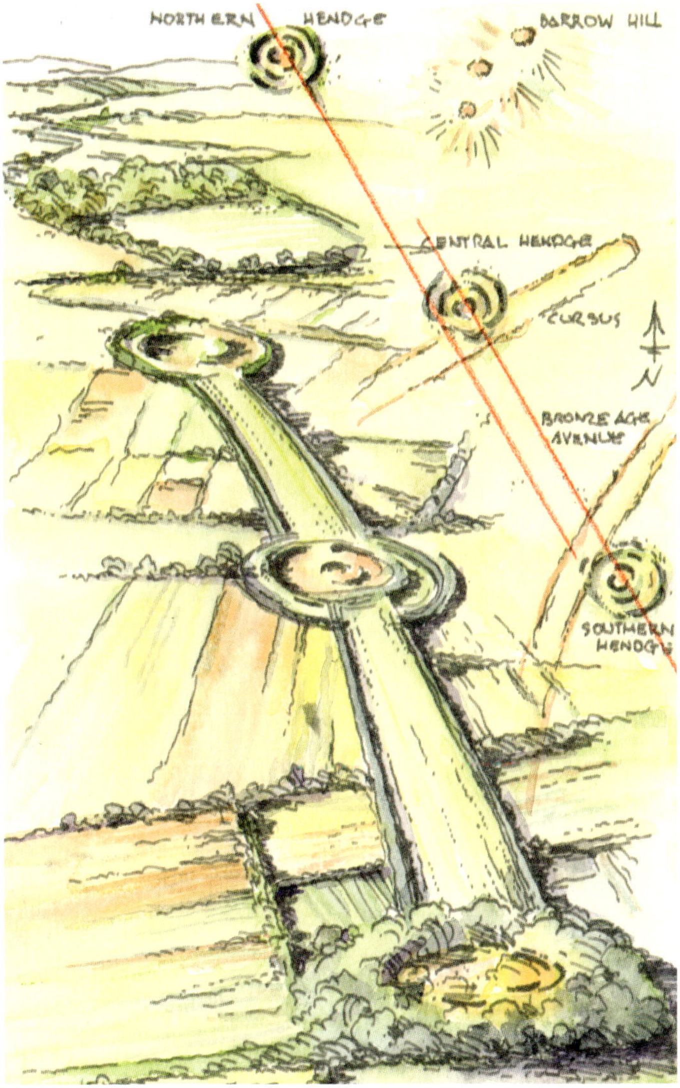
NORTHERN HENDGE
BARROW HILL
CENTRAL HENDGE
CURSUS
N
BRONZE AGE AVENUE
SOUTHERN HENDGE

HENGES

THE OMPHALOS

The human navel marks the spot where one's umbilical cord was detached at birth, a scar from where we were untethered from our mothers. Medically, our navel is referenced as the center point of our abdominal quadrants. The earth also has a center point, or zero point, where the equator meets the prime meridian, and divides the globe into four hemispheres. Located in the Gulf of Guinea, nearest to Ghana, the imaginary "Null Island" lies at the point of 0° latitude and 0° longitude. But does the Earth have a navel?

Omphalos is the Greek word for navel. In Greek mythology, Zeus released two eagles from opposite ends of the Earth; they met at Delphi where a stone was raised, establishing the city as the center of the world. The conical-shaped stone is called the *omphalos*. Similarly shaped stones, petroglyphs, and tomb paintings, some dating from the neolithic era, appear throughout Eastern Europe and Egypt, although their symbolism has not been connected to the idea of omphalos.

Delphi is not the only place believed to be the center of the world. Cusco, the capital of the Inca Empire, means "navel of the earth" in Quechua. The city of Prayagraj, located at the confluence of the Ganga and Yamuna rivers in India, is a sacred Hindu pilgrimage site from where Brahma chose to create the universe. In Ancestral Puebloan culture the sipapu, or small round pit excavated within the floor of a kiva, is the symbolic point of origin, or portal, through which humans first climbed into the world. Omphalos signifies the idea of centering and emergence, a connection to the earth that is critical to maintain.

VIII

THE OMPHALOS

BRIDGES

Metaphorically, a bridge is a connection between two worlds: the known and the unknown. It can also represent the beginning of a journey and the necessity of making a choice or a life-changing decision to cross over to the other side. The bridge is often the symbol for crossing into a magical realm.

A perfect example of a faerie bridge can be found in the remote landscape of Glen Creran in Scotland's West Highlands. Finding this bridge can take great effort as it is not on any of the major trails. Just as one gives up hope, it magically appears: a diminutive, arched stone bridge with strangely upturned, sharply pointed, stone balustrades spanning a deep brook of crystal-clear water. It is said that once you cross this bridge you will not be the same person you were when you took your first step across. The pointed shards of stone seem weirdly like the crown of a troll.

Trolls seem to be drawn to stone bridges and sometimes even become part of the bridge itself. Why do trolls linger under bridges and demand a toll or token for crossing? What does this represent? Perhaps a troll demands a token to allow you the privilege of embarking on a journey into the unknown. We can never know what awaits us on the other side and, thus, making an offering becomes an important part of this ritual procession.

We are crossing bridges constantly in our harried modern lives. Perhaps, before we pass over, we should pause for a moment and contemplate their metaphysical meaning. Just maybe we might be able to enter that magic realm on the other side.

IX

BRIDGES

MOUNDS

To dig and to pile are basic human compulsions. Throughout time people have used the earth to make and mark space. Human-made earthworks symbolize the spirit of the natural forms they imitate. Pyramids and ziggurats are stairways to heaven, evocative of sacred mountains; geoglyphs and effigy mounds take the shape of sacred animals, linking their spirit with the land. A mound can function as a platform to attain elevation, a solid base with no interior; equally, the form may contain space, include an interior chamber, and function as a burial site. We raise mounds also to mark time, to hold back water, and to create arable land. *Chinampas* are a great example of traditional wisdom—using dredge to raise "floating islands" for agricultural purposes—applied to a contemporary context.

There are many earth mound sites across the Midwest that date from the ancient Adena, Hopewell, and Mississippian periods. The Cahokia Mounds, near present day St. Louis, are the largest prehistoric earthworks in the Americas, on par with better known sites in Mexico and Central America. Cahokia was a thriving economic and religious center of Mississippian culture in the eleventh century. The 4,000-acre site was laid out in a grid, roughly aligned with sunrise at summer solstice. The largest earthwork is Monks Mound, a 14-acre terraced platform mound. Serpent Mound, in southern Ohio, is believed to be the largest prehistoric effigy mound in the world. The head of the quarter-mile-long earthwork, shaped like a snake, aligns with sunset at summer solstice; there is speculation about the body and tail of the serpent marking other astronomical alignments.

X
MOUNDS

HEDGE WITCHES

Historically a hedge witch was a witch who was not a member of a coven and lived at the edge of the known world and the wilderness, beyond the hedge on the outskirts of town. As an inhabitant of the outskirts, the hedge witch was an intermediary between civilization and the natural world. More often women than men, hedge witches were healers, shamans, and keepers of extensive botanical knowledge of herbs and medicines. Much of their time was spent collecting plants and herbs and then using their home as a lab to analyze, study, and classify the effects of plants. The home was a workplace for study and a center for magical activity. Bookshelves were full of ancient magical texts, amulets, curative potions, and spells. Everywhere you looked plants accumulated in various stages of preparation for curatives. Detailed journals held records of the processes, recipes, and discoveries. The practice of the hedge witch was deeply personal and held a sincere reverence for nature; it was a journey grounded in the communion of the spirits of place.

The popularity of the *Harry Potter* films might foretell the dawn of a new age—an invitation to positive associations with the magical arts. There is a resurgence in the community of hedge witches in contemporary paganism. Today's hedge witch is usually self-taught and self-motivated and not part of a broader ideology or dogma. To become a hedge witch you must first learn the medicinal and spiritual properties of everything that grows. A wise hedge witch enlists nature; we would do well to follow that advice.

XI
HEDGE WITCHES

ASASE YAA

Asase Yaa is the female spirit of the earth and the goddess of agriculture and fertility to the Indigenous Akan and Ashanti people of West Africa. Her name combines the words for "Earth" (*asase*) and "Thursday" (*yaa*) the day the earth was believed to be created, and hence the day that the earth must remain undisturbed and allowed to rest. There are no burials on Thursdays. Asase Yaa is venerated in tilled soil and plowed fields. Working a field is a sacred act. Prior to any excavation or agitation of the earth, a libation must be poured to seek permission to perform the work.

The Ashanti people of Ghana represent a matrilineal society. *Asantehemaa* is the title given to Queen Mothers, women elders who offer their counsel and wisdom to the community's leaders. The concepts of stewardship and motherhood extend to attitudes and values toward the land. At death, Asase Yaa reclaims her children and, in asking her to accept the return of her people, a libation is offered. Similarly, at birth, when a child is placed on a mat on the ground as part of a naming ceremony called an "outdooring," offerings of gratitude along with prayers for protection from the ancestral guardians are made to Asase Yaa.

Asase Yaa is also associated with truth and virtue. Her people are custodians of the land; land is not a commodity to be bought or sold, and people have a responsibility to keep the earth clean.

XII
ASASE YAA

THE PERSIAN CARPET

The Persian Carpet originated more than 2,500 years ago in Iran and was initially woven as articles of necessity to cover the floors of the nomadic peoples' tents. These carpets were originally created not only as a floor covering for warmth and comfort, but also as a decorative design that could be contemplated and enjoyed. The garden carpet could be rolled up and taken with the tribe on their travels. As people migrated through the harsh desert, a portion of a garden paradise travelled with them.

By the 17th-century in Iran, the garden carpet became a highly valued art form. Many beautiful and intricate garden carpets were woven, some so life-like that one would hardly believe they had not entered paradise. These designs were based on the Persian four-square garden with waterways and lush plantations filled with an amazing variety of wildlife, waterfowl, tiny insects, and even snails. This profusion of foliage and blossoms is depicted with intricate abstract patterns creating infinitely repeating designs. When gazing at the carpet from above and studying this aerial perspective, you get the sensation of flying atop the landscape. Another interesting effect can be achieved as you imagine yourself shrinking down to the scale of the garden and experiencing it in real time.

Looking at the garden carpet for long periods of time can also have a hallucinogenic effect, transporting you into another dimension. These richly intricate floral designs and patterns will begin to explode with radiating psychedelic colors. Perhaps this effect is the origins of the legendary "flying carpet," a mystical opportunity to transport us to almost anywhere imaginable.

XIII

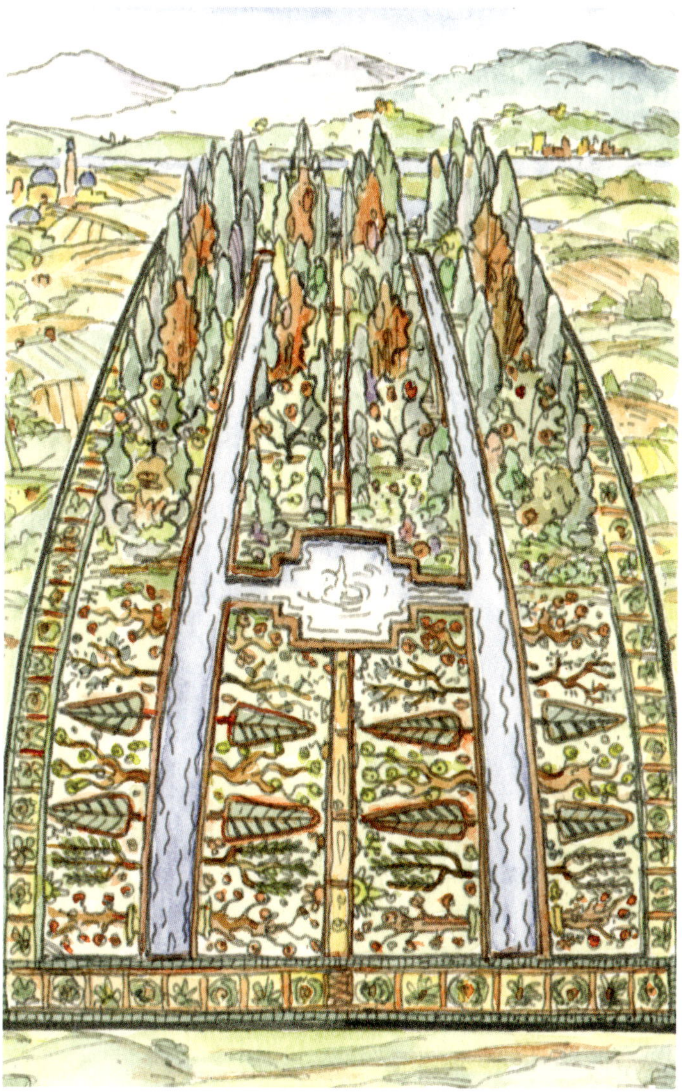

THE PERSIAN CARPET

HORTUS CONCLUSUS

A *hortus conclusus* is a walled or enclosed garden. The form is representative of medieval gardens in western Europe, a time and place when the landscape was held suspect, perceived as a wild and fearful place. Walled gardens represented security, a place of cultivation and care, a paradise if you will; this association with the ideal of a balanced and harmonious world inspires us. The *hortus conclusus*, as a tended garden, is a fine metaphor with which to conclude our survey of sacred landscape archetypes.

The *hortus conclusus*, the pleasance, and the monastic cloister garden are all characteristic forms of medieval gardens. Common attributes of a *hortus conclusus* include a wall or fence, the geometric subdivision of raised planting beds, turf seats, a well or fountain, and grass or flowery mead. Depictions of medieval walled gardens are frequently laden with Christian religious symbolism. Nestled within the walls of castles, *pleasance* (or pleasure) gardens are associated with the cult of chivalry and knighthood that emerged in the Middle Ages. Elaborate pleasance gardens might include labyrinths, mounts, topiary, and even menageries. The cloister garden is similar in form to the peristyle garden of the Roman *domus*—a colonnaded ambulatory surrounding a typically square courtyard with a central basin or fountain, a place for reflection.

In a sense the planet Earth is a *hortus conclusus*. The biosphere exists as a closed system, only energy in the form of radiation from the sun is transferred outside the system, not matter. In the Anthropocene era, human actions have altered the Earth's self-regulating systems. We must work to restore the sanctuary of our planetary *hortus conclusus*.

XIV

HORTUS CONCLUSUS

CONCLUSION

Wisdom of Place represents a visual dialog in which Chip and Elizabeth explore the spiritual relationships between people and nature, between past and present, myth and metaphor, self and world. In conclusion, we ask you to add your creative voice to the conversation and express how you experience the *genius loci*. Our conclusion is your beginning.

The tarot offers a way to start a dialog; it is what you want it to be. And like the landscape, the tarot is alive, it is a medium of exchange. To create is to make a connection, to find patterns, associations, and affinities, where none existed before. We hope that you found inspiration in our interpretations of how the earth holds knowledge, and that you continue your search for the sacredness in the landscapes that surround you.

0

YOUR CARD HERE

BIBLIOGRAPHY

Booth, Mark. *The Illustrated Secret History of the World*. NY: Overlook Press, 2018.

Campbell, Joseph. *Goddesses: Mysteries of the Feminine Divine.* Novato, CA: New World Library, 2013.

Chatwin, Bruce. *The Songlines*. NY: Penguin Books, 1987.

Crispin, Jessa. *The Creative Tarot: A Modern Guide to an Inspired Life*. NY: Atria/Simon & Schuster, 2016.

Dell, Christopher. *The Occult, Witchcraft and Magic: An Ilustrated History*. NY: Thames and Hudson, 2016.

Evans-Wentz, W.Y. *The Fairy-Faith in Celtic Countries*. Franklin Lakes, NJ: New Page Books, 2004.

Fiebig, Johannes and Evelin Burger. *The Ultimate Guide to the Rider Waite Tarot.* Woodbury, MN: Llewelyn Publications, 2017.

Fontana, David. *The Secret Language of Symbols: A Visual Key to Symbols and Their Meanings*. SF: Chronicle Books, 1994.

Frazer, James G. *The Golden Bough: The Roots of Religion and Folklore*. NY: Avenel Books, 1981.

Giesecke, Annette. *The Mythology of Plants*. Los Angeles, CA: J. Paul Getty Museum, 2014.

Giles, Cynthia. *The Tarot: History, Mystery and Lore*. NY: Fireside/Simon & Schuster, 1992.

Graves, Robert. *The White Goddess: A Historical Grammar of Poetic Myth*. NY: Farrar Straus Giroux, 1997.

Hamilton, Edith. *Mythology: Timeless Tales of Gods and Heroes*. NY: Mentor Books/ New American Library, 1963.

Huntley, H.E. *The Divine Proportion: A Study in Mathematical Beauty*. NY: Dover Publications, 1970.

Lawlor, Robert. *Sacred Geometry: Philosophy and Practice*. NY: Thames and Hudson, 1982.

Michell, John. *The View Over Atlantis*. NY: Ballantine Books Inc., 1973

Michell, John. *The Earth Spirit: Its Ways, Shrines and Mysteries*. NY: Avon Books, 1975.

Monaghan, *Patricia. Encyclopedia of Goddesses and Heroines*. Novato, CA: New World Library, 2014.

Muten, Burleigh. *Goddesses: A World of Myth and Magic.* Cambridge, MA: Barefoot Books, 2003.

New York Historical Society Museum and Library. *Harry Potter: A History of Magic*. NY: Arthur A. Levine Books/Scholastic Inc., 2018.

Niebel, Jessica, et al. *Hayao Miyazaki*. Los Angeles, CA: Academy Museum of Motion Pictures and DelMonico Books, 2021.

Odum, Howard T. *Environment, Power and Society*. NY: John Wiley and Sons, 1971.

Pennick, Nigel. *The Pagan Book of Days.* Rochester, VT: Destiny Books, 1992.

Revenson, Jody. *Harry Potter: The Artifact Vault*. San Rafael, CA: Insight Editions, 2016.

Robinette, Gary. *Plants, People and Environmental Quality*. National Park Service/US Department of the Interior, 1972.

Schama, Simon. *Landscape and Memory.* Toronto, Canada: Vintage Canada Edition/Alfred A. Knopf, 1996.

Sofroniew, Alexandra. *Household Gods: Private Devotion in Ancient Greece and Rome*. Los Angeles, CA: J. Paul Getty Museum, 2015.

Studio Ghibli. *Princess Mononoke: The Art and Making of Japan's Most Popular Film of All Time*. NY: Hyperion, 1997.

Yeats, W.B. *The Celtic Twilight: Faerie and Folklore*. Mineola, NY: Dover Publications, 2004.